The Evolution of Media

The Evolution of Media

A. MICHAEL NOLL

ROWMAN & LITTLEFIELD PUBLISHERS, INC.
Lanham • Boulder • New York • Toronto • Plymouth, UK

ROWMAN & LITTLEFIELD PUBLISHERS, INC.

Published in the United States of America
by Rowman & Littlefield Publishers, Inc.
A wholly owned subsidiary of The Rowman & Littlefield Publishing Group, Inc.
4501 Forbes Boulevard, Suite 200, Lanham, Maryland 20706
www.rowmanlittlefield.com

Estover Road, Plymouth PL6 7PY, United Kingdom

British Library Cataloguing in Publication Information Available

Library of Congress Cataloging-in-Publication Data

Noll, A. Michael.
    The evolution of media / A. Michael Noll.
      p. cm.
    Includes bibliographical references and index.
    ISBN-13: 978-0-7425-5481-8 (cloth : alk. paper)
    ISBN-10: 0-7425-5481-3 (cloth : alk. paper)
    ISBN-13: 978-0-7425-5482-5 (pbk. : alk. paper)
    ISBN-10: 0-7425-5482-1 (pbk. : alk. paper)
    1. Mass media and technology—History. I. Title.
P96.T42N65 2006
302.2309—dc22
                                    2006024496

Printed in the United States of America

♾ The paper used in this publication meets the minimum requirements of American National Standard for Information Sciences–Permanence of Paper for Printed Library Materials, ANSI/NISO Z39.48-1992.

To Peter Clarke, for his vision in shaping the study of communication and for guiding my career in the academic world.

Contents

Preface

This book is a guide to the exciting and challenging world of communication media. Exciting because of all the many technologies that enable a wide variety of communication in many different forms. Challenging in trying to make some sense of the variety of media and in creating a framework to help understand the future of communication.

Various forms of communication media, including their historical development, are described in this book to give a broad perspective of their variety and utility. Communication media are compared in terms of their various dimensions, such as modality, purpose, interactivity, capacity, and technological requirements. A taxonomy of communication media is developed. Conclusions and general observations are made about the significant characteristics and dimensions of communication media. Lastly, a methodology is presented for analyzing strategic dimensions to identify those most significant in determining the likelihood of success of a communication service or product.

This book serves two purposes. One purpose is to introduce communication students to the world of communication media and to stimulate them to think about how media might evolve in the future. A second purpose is to provide people in the communication industry with an overall framework for comparing media and the means for identifying, analyzing, and evaluating opportunities for new communication products and services.

There is considerable hype and overpromotion of many supposedly new communication services and products. This book is not intended to provide answers to which specific ones will succeed, but does provide a methodology and the ways and means for analyzing and understanding communication services and products. As an example, satellite radio is being heavily promoted, but its ultimate success remains unclear. The perspective developed in this book would emphasize that satellite radio is still radio—namely, audio delivered to a mass market—and the satellite is only a technological transmission medium.

But the real objective of this book is to encourage the reader to think about the various dimensions and factors that can be used to characterize communication media.

This book has had a long history. It began with some early work performed with the support of Eugene S. Miller of the NYNEX Corporation in the late 1980s. The first draft was written during 1990 and 1991 while I was on sabbatical from the Annenberg School for Communication at the University of Southern California. A rough manuscript was then used for an undergraduate seminar that was conducted during both the 1996 and 1997 spring semesters at the Annenberg School. Additional editorial effort went into creating yet another manuscript of the book during yet another sabbatical in the fall of 1998. Editorial revisions were made from 1999 through 2002, resulting in a version that was accepted for publication by Burnham Inc. Publishers, but Burnham was dissolved during the editing of the manuscript before it could be published. Burnham's assets were then acquired by Rowman & Littlefield, and additional revision of the manuscript was made before it was finally submitted again for publication, after nearly two decades of gestation.

A number of friends and colleagues commented on drafts of the book, and their comments and other interactions helped me refine my ideas. I appreciate all their assistance, but I particularly want to thank Dr. Martin C. J. Elton and Dr. William H. Dutton. In particular, Dr. Elton encouraged me to continue working on this book when I began to doubt that I would ever be able to make sense of the world of communication media, and his enthusiasm and wise counsel continued thereafter to the last drafts. Professors Peter Clarke and Everett M. Rogers commented on early drafts of the book and helped guide my preliminary thoughts.

1

Introduction

COMMUNICATION

Communication makes us human. We express our thoughts, our ideas, and our emotions through communication. Deprived of communication, we become isolated, lonely, and depressed. Communication is our way of reaching other persons through such ways as a warm touch, a fleeting glance, or a kind word.

Human communication has been augmented and extended over physical distance through communication media, such as books, letters, the telephone, broadcast television, and the Internet. The term *media* has acquired its own significance, including the industry that packages and presents information to us through the printed words of the newspaper, the spoken words of radio, and the visual imagery of television. But communication media also include such electronic, interpersonal forms as the telephone, cell phone, telegraph, facsimile, and the e-mails of the Internet. Thus, communication media are all encompassing and include broadcast and interpersonal media, physically delivered and telecommunicated media, paper-based and electronic media, and the many transmission media that carry telecommunication signals.

The communication industry in the United States accounts for about 7 percent of the gross national product. We cannot escape being touched daily by the communication industry. On the average we spend six hours per day watching television and make seven telephone calls per day. Some of us spend an hour or more each day on the Internet—perhaps the most dramatic growth medium of today.

1

COMMUNICATION DEFINED

Communication can be defined as the exchange, interchange, or transmission of messages. Communication can occur for many purposes. Most communication occurs because the content of the communication—the message—is intended either to inform or to entertain, or sometimes both. The message is the content of communication. That message is carried over some conduit— the medium—of communication.

Moving images and sound, intended to inform or entertain, are the content of television. The signals that make up television are carried to homes over the coaxial cable of CATV, broadcast to homes over the air by radio waves from terrestrial antennas and from communication satellites, or physically carried to homes on videocassettes and disks rented and purchased from a video store. Some day in the future, video entertainment might be accessed over the Internet.

The terms *communication medium* and *media* have a number of meanings and can apply to television itself, to the whole news and entertainment industry, or to the specific technological conduit used to convey TV signals. Since all these different meanings are explored in this book, we need to start by defining what is meant by communication media. This introductory discussion begins with a general model of the overall process of communication—a model known as *Shannon's model of communication*.

SHANNON'S MODEL OF COMMUNICATION

In communication engineering, Claude E. Shannon is known for his detailed mathematical analyses of the capacity of a communication channel. In social-sciences communication, Claude E. Shannon is known for his overall model of the communication process (Shannon 1948). This model actually forms the overall framework for his detailed mathematical analyses of communication, which are used in communication engineering. The Shannon model of communication consists simply of a source, channel, and destination, as shown in figure 1.1. The source includes some form of transmitter, and the destination includes some form of receiver. The channel is corrupted by the presence of noise.

The source generates a message that is then encoded for transmission by the transmitter. The message generated by the source could be the symbols from

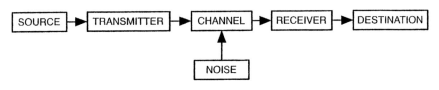

FIGURE 1.1
Shannon's model of a communication system

a Teletype machine, the electrical signal from a telephone, or the signal from a TV camera. The source in Shannon's model is a communication machine of some kind—not a human being. The human in the process is behind the source, and accordingly Shannon's model and theory of communication does not apply to the meaning and emotion of communication. Hence, Shannon's detailed mathematical analyses pertain only to certain very specific types of signals. Nevertheless, Shannon's work has been misinterpreted and misapplied to virtually every form of human communication, including art and music.

Although many social-science communication scholars know about Shannon's overall model of the communication process, Shannon's real contribution was not this model but the mathematical theory of communication he developed using the model as an overall framework. His theory deals with the capacity of a communication channel and a measure of the information content of a signal, called *entropy*. Shannon performed a mathematical analysis of communication in the presence of noise. He showed that perfect reception was possible under certain conditions. Shannon's theories showed the way for the development of error-correcting codes. One application of such codes is the compact disc (CD) used for audio. The error-correcting codes used in the CD are able to correct perfectly as much as an eighth of an inch of any obscured portion along the signal track of the CD.

COMMUNICATION MEDIA

According to Shannon, communication involves a channel of some kind. That channel is carried over some medium. In Shannon's model, that medium was typically a pair of copper wires or a portion of the radio spectrum. But *medium* can have other meanings too, and in the spirit world, a medium acts as an intermediary between the living person and the dead spirit.

A medium of communication comes between the source and intended recipient of the communication. The medium conveys or carries the communication. A newspaper reporter writes a story. That story is printed in the newspaper, which is then physically delivered to the recipient. The newspaper—consisting of the printed word on paper—is the communication medium.

Communication may be a one-way process in which the content is sent from one source to many recipients, such as by radio or television. Such communication from one to many is called *broadcast*. Since the content of broadcast communication is usually intended for many recipients who form a large (or mass) audience, such communication is also called *mass communication*. Radio, television, newspapers, and magazines are all part of the mass communication industry—also known as *mass media*, or more simply, as *the media*.

Communication can also be a two-way process between only two persons, such as by the telephone. A person makes a telephone call to a distant friend. The telephone system—consisting of the telephone instruments, various transmission technologies, and switching machines—is the medium of communication between the two persons speaking. Such communication from one person to another is called *interpersonal*. The two-way nature of most interpersonal communication is an interactive process, and the media used for such communication are called *interactive media*. The telephone system is a two-way, interactive, interpersonal communication medium. Today, many other media are also called *interactive*, but whether they are truly two-way is sometimes less clear. Communication over an electronic medium is sometimes called *mediated communication*.

THE MEDIA

When we speak of *the media*, we are usually referring to the press, including newspapers, magazines, television, and radio. But should other mass communication media, such as motion pictures and compact discs, be included? Should the term *mass media* include all media that are disseminated to a mass audience, including audio compact discs and digital video discs, which are delivered physically? Different people use these terms quite differently.

The term *the media* will be used in this book to refer to the news media. This includes newspapers, magazines, television, and radio, since all these communication media prepare and disseminate news. The term *mass media* will refer to all communication media that disseminate information of any kind and for any purpose to a mass audience.

Does it make sense to use the term *mass media* to refer to compact discs? The delay between production and distribution of these discs and the individualized nature of the listening experience seem to exclude the use of *mass medium* for compact discs. Furthermore, how should a telephone service that allows a large number of people to receive the same recorded message, such as weather or time, be classified? Is this an interpersonal, or a mass, medium?

And what about the term *new media*? What does it mean? At one time, many years ago, the term *new media* included computers used to send text messages from one person to another. But that form of electronic mail is no longer new. Another term in use today is *emerging technologies*. It too is nebulous in meaning, particularly since most communication technologies progressively evolve and emerge from existing technologies.

These terms are indeed confusing. One purpose of this book is to illuminate what is meant by communication media by describing all the forms in detail. Various ways to classify and understand the uses and characteristics of different media are presented to clarify and illuminate the breadth of the world of communication media.

COMMUNICATION MODALITIES

Language is one means of communication. It consists of a body of signs and symbols—spoken, written, and graphic—by which we communicate with each other. These signs and symbols are communicated in a wide variety of ways, known as modalities. Much communication involves visual imagery of various kinds, such as written characters and drawings. Sound, such as human speech, is another important modality for communication.

Communication, however, extends far beyond spoken and written language. Music certainly is a form of artistic communication, as is painting. Motion pictures and television are means of video communication. Newspapers, magazines, and letters communicate through the written word. Photographs and paintings are graphic means of communication. The fictitious "feelie" of Aldous Huxley's *Brave New World* and some portions of virtual reality are means of tactual communication. These different modalities of communication can be carried over a variety of communication media.

MEDIA-RICH HOME

A tremendous number and variety of communication media are available for the home—so many, that one wonders whether there is room for anything else. Radio waves deliver VHF and UHF television, AM and FM radio, two-way radio, direct broadcast satellite (DBS) television, and microwave TV. Television is also delivered to the home over the coaxial cable of the CATV firm. TV shows may be recorded at home on the videocassette recorder (VCR) for later viewing, and digital video discs (DVD) are brought home from the video store for viewing on the home TV set. In Europe and many other parts of the world, frames of information consisting of text and graphics are broadcast along with the TV signal and can be displayed on the TV set—a service called *teletext*.

The telephone makes possible two-way interpersonal communication, and the switched telephone network can also be used with a modem to give the home computer user access to the Internet to surf remote databases and to send and receive text messages. High-speed access to the Internet occurs via cable modems connected to the coaxial cable of CATV or over DSL (digital subscriber line) modems connected to the telephone line.

The home answer-and-record machine takes voice messages when no one is at home or wants to answer the phone. The home computer can be used with disks to access large files of information. The home stereo is used with digital audio compact discs and audiocassettes. Books, magazines, mail, and a host of other electronic media are physically delivered to the home. Cellular radio enables use of the phone when on the road and also helps direct lost delivery trucks to the home.

In the future, optical fiber promises even more television programming, perhaps even individual shows on demand. Coaxial cable is used to broadcast television programming and is made two-way for data access to the Internet through use of a cable modem. The coaxial cable can even be used to carry telephone conversations in competition with the twisted pair of copper wires provided by the local telephone company.

All these communication media in the home cluster about four centers: the video entertainment center (television), the audio entertainment center (hi-fi or stereo), the communication center (corded and cordless telephones and the answering machine), and the home computer center (the personal computer). The home computer center is relatively new and includes the personal computer (used initially as a word processor replacement for the typewriter

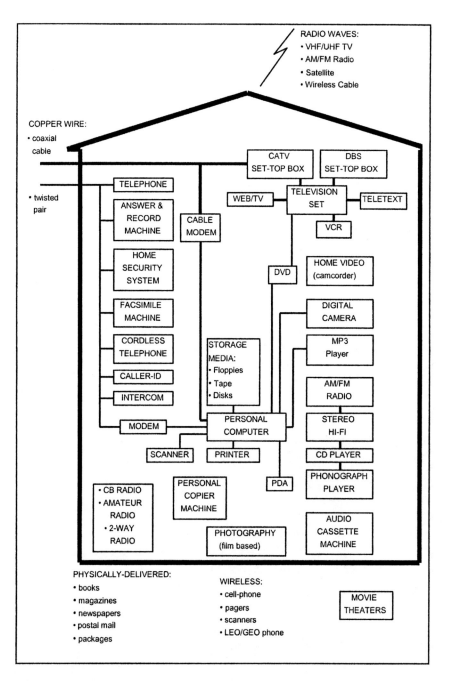

FIGURE 1.2
Media-rich home

and increasingly to manage a variety of digital media), a home copier, and a home facsimile machine. The four centers have been quite distinct, although some futurists believe that some of the centers might converge. However, most people still seem to want to keep work separate from play. Yet the personal computer has increasingly become central to the storage and creation of digital media, such as digital camcorders, digital cameras, and compressed digital audio (such as MP3 music players and Apple's series of iPod music and video players).

OFFICE COMMUNICATION

Electronic communication media have had a big impact at the office. Desks are so crowded with electronic media that there scarcely is room for a pen and pencil. The telephone may include a speakerphone for hands-free use and for small-group conferencing. A repertory dialer speeds calls to frequently dialed numbers. The facsimile unit enables letters to be sent instantly and is indispensable for telecommunication overseas. The personal computer is used for word processing and spreadsheet analyses. The laptop computer is carried back and forth between home and the office.

Personal digital assistants (PDAs) are used to manage contacts and appointments. The small PDA portable unit connects to personal computers so that information can be synchronized between the two machines. The personal digital assistant replaces the paper address book and calendar, and wireless PDAs give access to e-mail while on the move.

The corporate telecommunication network is extensive. Customers call using toll-free 800 numbers. Teleconferencing facilities facilitate group meetings, and closed-circuit video is used by chief executives to reach employees scattered throughout the country. Text messages are sent by electronic mail (e-mail) over the Internet and internal packet-switched networks (Intranets). The local telephone system includes voice-mail services to take messages and to speed connections to the appropriate party. The future holds promise for an integration of voice, data, and graphic telecommunication through an integrated services digital network (ISDN) in which all signals are in digital form.

MEDIA PROGRESSION AND REPLACEMENT

Communication media have progressed over time through various technological innovations and improvements. Cave drawings and stone tablets were

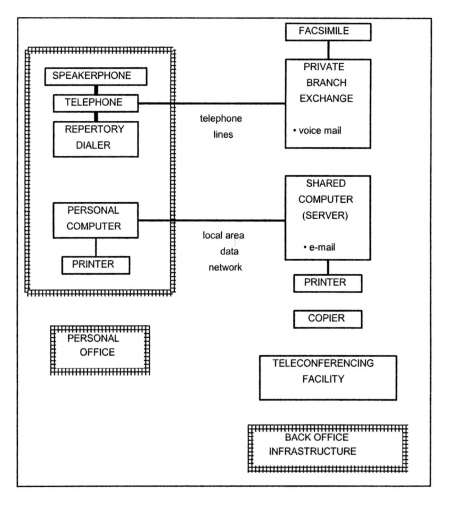

FIGURE 1.3
Office media

replaced by papyrus and paper. The printing press mechanized the production of books and led to newspapers and magazines. Drums, carrier pigeons, and human runners enabled communication over distance, and instantaneous communication over greater distances was accomplished with electricity and radio. Music can be recorded and distributed on discs or tapes and broadcast over radio waves. Motion pictures are a source of entertainment and can be viewed in the movie theater or on television. At one time, it was predicted that television would replace the movie theater, but we now know that television and movie theaters coexist. The newer medium did not replace the older medium. Similarly, FM radio did not replace the older AM radio; the two media coexist with their own distinct program formats and audiences. Nor has CATV or DBS yet replaced over-the-air VHF/UHF television, although the percentage of homes that obtain television over the conduit of VHF/UHF airwaves is dwindling.

However, a newer medium can sometimes replace an older one. For example, compact discs have replaced vinyl phonograph records. However, the argument can be made that the medium—recorded audio—is the same and only the technological conduit or process has changed. But then the coaxial cable of CATV is only a conduit compared to the airwaves of VHF/UHF television, and given the large proportion of homes in the United States that receive television either by CATV or DBS, perhaps the death of over-the-air VHF/UHF television will occur someday soon. The subject of media progression and replacement clearly is complex, and care should be exercised in making sweeping generalizations.

PROCESS/MEDIUM

The communication process is frequently intertwined with the medium. The compact disc uses a digital process to store recorded sound. However, the medium is still the recording of audio. The process involves technology, and newer technologies replace older technologies. The new digital process of the compact disc has clearly replaced the older analog process of the 33⅓ rpm phonograph record.

What exactly is the communication medium? Are motion pictures the same medium as television since both deal with moving images? Is television simply a technological improvement over movies? Probably not, since movies are intended to be viewed in a movie theater with many people simultaneously sharing an experience, while television is beamed to individual homes. Motion pictures could be distributed electronically to movie theaters. The medium would be the same, but the process would be changed from physical film to an electronic form.

THE MEDIUM IS THE MESSAGE

The Canadian communication scholar Marshall McLuhan made the profound observation that "the medium is the message." What he meant was that the choice of medium itself sends a message to the recipient. McLuhan then characterized various media as ranging from "hot" to "cool." McLuhan observed that "all media are extensions of some human faculty—psychic or physical" (McLuhan and Fiore 1962, 26). McLuhan's interest in communication was stimulated by the Canadian economist Harold Innis, who observed that modern communication electronics increase speed and distance, and warned how this could cause cultural disturbances and favor centralization and bureaucracy, resulting in "monopolies in the field of knowledge" (Innis 1951, 31, 82, and 190).

ISOLATION
Communication media have created a means for people to be physically isolated yet remain in touch with friends through such interpersonal telecommunication as the telephone and cell phone, and in touch with the world through the collective experience of television. A Sony Walkman cassette or CD player and the Apple iPod allow people to listen to music wherever they may be, but they also isolate people from their surroundings in situations that otherwise seem too public, such as a busy subway train or a crowded street.

OVERVIEW OF BOOK
Clearly, communication is a complex and broad topic, challenging to comprehend and understand fully. The whole field of communication is so vast that most people are overwhelmed and baffled in their attempts to predict its future, but they wonder what new services and products will succeed in the marketplace. This book attempts to provide the knowledge, broad perspective, distinctions, and methodology necessary to understand communication media—now and in the future.

This understanding is fostered by first describing the many different mass and interpersonal communication media and their history. Mass media—such as radio, television, and newspapers—are treated first, followed by interpersonal media—such as the telephone. The treatment is mostly descriptive.

Because technology has played an important role in the history and development of most communication media, I firmly believe that a basic understanding of the fundamentals of technology is essential. Hence, many of the key technological principles are covered in short tutorials combined together in an appendix.

The descriptions of various communication media form the first part of this book. The second part is a comparative analysis of these media. The comparative analysis starts with the introduction of a taxonomy for the classification and comparison of media. The many dimensions of the taxonomy are used to compare media and to understand the many uses of media, today and tomorrow. The taxonomy and classification methods are applied to various communication media in the third part of the book. Along the way, some general conclusions, and possibly a theory or two, are developed. The taxonomy is intended to foster discussion by creating a framework to attempt to organize and characterize communication media, rather than a rigid and definite classification scheme that will never work because many media cross boundaries. The fourth and last part of this book presents a simple framework for analyzing products and services to determine their likelihood of success.

Some aspects of communication media are controversial, particularly those aspects that deal with markets and uses. For example, video telephones have consistently failed, but nevertheless some people believe that new technology will make them affordable to all and such telephones will then succeed. Video telephones have failed in the marketplace because most people simply have no need or desire to see the other person—or to be seen—while using the telephone. Hence the video telephone will continue to fail in the marketplace, regardless of new technological developments. Yet new video telephones continue to be developed and marketed each year, some using personal computers and wireless appliances.

My personal biases and opinions are sprinkled throughout this book. I hope you will recognize them as such, and develop your own views and opinions. I ask only that you base your opinions on an understanding of the past and try to learn the lessons from the history of past mistakes—and also the successes.

REFERENCES

Innis, Harold A. *The Bias of Communication*. Toronto: University of Toronto Press, 1951.

McLuhan, Marshall. *Understanding Media: The Extensions of Man*. New York: McGraw Hill, 1964. Reprinted by MIT Press, 1994.

McLuhan, Marshall, and Quentin Fiore. *The Medium Is the Massage: An Inventory of Effects*. New York: Bantam Books, 1962.

Shannon, Claude E. "A Mathematical Theory of Communication." *Bell System Technical Journal* 27 (1948): 379–423, 623–656.

I

UNDERSTANDING COMMUNICATION MEDIA

The first part of this book describes the various ways in which communication can occur. Many communication media can be categorized as broadcast or interpersonal, but the boundaries between the two categories are blurry, and overlaps occur. Broadcast media send information to a large number of recipients, usually in one direction, from the source to many receivers. Interpersonal communication media are usually two-way, between two participants.

Communication media are described in the following chapters according to the modality of the medium. Broadcast and interpersonal media are organized into three modalities: (1) the written and printed word, (2) audio, and (3) still and moving images. The descriptions of various communication media include their history and their key inventors. The problem is that many media do not fall nicely into categories, but a book requires an organized flow—one that hopefully is not too forced or haphazard.

The Written Word: From Printing to the Internet

GENESIS OF THE WRITTEN WORD

The grunts and groans of early humans evolved into an elaborate series of sounds that could be used for communication. Human speech and its system of language are unique in their flexibility to convey all sorts of emotions, ideas, and concepts. However, human speech exists in time and is thus not preserved without the use of some form of technology, such as paper and the printing press. Thus the history of the past could only be saved through memorization and passed on through oral tradition. This situation changed with the invention of writing—first on clay tablets and then on paper. Newspapers enabled the printed word to be broadcast to many people.

The most customary form of interpersonal communication is face-to-face between two or more persons. In face-to-face communication we may see, hear, smell, touch, and experience the physical presence of another person. It is truly an intimate experience between the persons. But physical presence is not always possible, and various communication media, starting with writing, have been invented to conquer distance and time for interpersonal communication.

The written word had its genesis in ancient cave paintings, which were attempts to convey ideas through pictures. Hieroglyphics, used by the Egyptians as early as 3000 BC, combined ideograms with symbols for syllables and single sounds. The modern Western alphabet evolved from written script used by the Sumerians at about the same time frame. Early writing was carved onto stone tablets or was inscribed into clay with a stylus. But such physical media were not easily transportable. This required a much lighter medium: paper.

Papyrus, formed from the stem of the papyrus plant, was invented and used by the Egyptians as early as 3000 BC. It was supplanted by the use of parchment, formed from animal skins. Paper, formed from a slurry of fibers in water, was first used by the Chinese as early as AD 100. The invention of the printing press enabled the mass distribution of the printed word. Much later, the invention of radio enabled the mass distribution of the spoken word.

Writing in all its forms was an important innovation for conquering distance and time. Messages could be recorded and delivered physically over great distances and could be saved for centuries. Space and time were conquered by the written word. However, physically delivering messages took time, and instantaneous real-time communication was not possible. The problem of physical delivery was conquered with the invention of telegraphy and its near-instantaneous transmission of electrical signals over great distances. But a special skill was needed to encode messages using Morse code for transmission over a telegraph communication system. That problem was solved ultimately by the invention of the telephone, which enabled two people to speak naturally to each other over great distances.

THE PRINTED WORD

Today, paper is the principal medium on which a message is carried in the form of the written or printed word. Long before paper and papyrus, messages had to be chiseled onto stone tablets, which were far too heavy to be carried over great distances. Although stone tablets were certainly a means of recording language, they were not a means for mass distribution.

The development of parchment, papyrus, and paper made the written word more accessible. But inscribing the message by hand was a very lengthy and time-consuming process, subject to copying errors. The solution was the invention of the printing press.

In the early fifteenth century, printing was accomplished by cutting the image into a block of wood that would then be inked. A piece of parchment or paper would then be pressed onto the wood block and would retain the inked image. The process was time-consuming and costly.

The solution was movable metal type, first used in Europe in 1439 by the German Johannes Gutenberg. In 1456, the Latin Bible was the first book to be printed with Gutenberg's movable metal type. However, we now know that movable type was used hundreds of years earlier in China and Korea.

In 1796, Aloys Senefelder in Munich invented lithography, a water/ink process. The technology of printing continued to progress. Photolithography was invented in France by Alfred Lemercier in 1852. The mechanical printing press was invented in 1803 in Germany by Friedrich Koenig. The first machine for making paper in long lengths was patented in 1799 by Nicholas-Louis Robert. The rotary printing press using a continuous roll of paper was patented in 1835 in Great Britain by Sir Rowland Hill. The linotype composing machine, invented by German-born Ottmar Mergenthaler working in the United States, was patented in 1885 and first used in 1886.

NEWSPAPERS AND MAGAZINES

Although newsletters and news pamphlets had appeared earlier, the first true newspapers appeared in the early 1600s. The earliest magazines appeared around 1670, and the first monthly magazine to use the term was *Gentleman's Magazine*, which was published in London beginning in 1731.

Today's newspapers and magazines are composed on electronic systems. Columnists and reporters write and enter their pieces directly at electronic display terminals, called video display terminals (VDT). They use personal computers at their desks or laptops for on the move. Newspapers today use color routinely, and some newspapers have achieved national distribution through the use of communication satellites that send the composed pages to printing locations throughout the United States.

Decades ago, radio was used to deliver newspapers, an early form of radio facsimile. The facsimile-delivered newspaper failed, perhaps because television broadcasting began at about the same time and was far more enjoyable to most consumers. Today, the Internet is being used to deliver newspapers and access news.

TYPEWRITERS

The use of the written and printed word as a communication medium was greatly facilitated by the invention of the typewriter. Typewriters of the past and their reincarnation as word processors are devices for the processing and encoding of alphanumeric symbols. The end result is still the written and printed word.

The typewriter traces its origins to a patent granted in 1714 to the Englishman Henry Mill. In 1874 in the United States, Christopher Sholes made the first commercially successful typewriter. The electric typewriter was introduced in the mid-1930s.

Yesterday's manual and electric typewriters have been replaced by the word processor. The word processor is a personal computer consisting of a keyboard and an electronic display screen, either a cathode ray tube (CRT) or a liquid crystal display (LCD). Corrections and editing are performed on the screen. The final copy is produced on a printer controlled by the word processor's computer. Printers have evolved from daisy-wheel impact machines to dot-matrix pin machines to very high-quality printers that use laser beams to draw characters on a drum in a xerographic process or that shoot colored inks through microscopic jets onto the paper.

COPIERS

The use of carbon paper to produce a copy of a typed document was commonplace for decades. Today, copies are made on copy machines that work on the xerographic process invented in 1938 by Chester Carlson in the United States. The first copiers based on the xerographic process were marketed in 1960. Modern copy machines are self-feeding and are able to collate and staple multiple copies automatically. Some can even create a booklet.

POSTAL SERVICE

With written language and lightweight writing instruments and surfaces, such as pen and paper, messages could be written and delivered to distant locations by postal service. Regular posts were made by the ancient Egyptians from 1600 to 1300 BC and in China from about 1000 BC. The modern postal service with its use of postage stamps and identical rates independent of distance within a country was formulated in 1840 in Great Britain by Sir Rowland Hill.

Physical delivery is required for postal service, and hence much time (with its inherent delay) is needed to transport a letter over great distances. The Pony Express began in 1860 and was able to carry mail over a distance of about nineteen hundred miles in ten days. It was a financial failure and was made obsolete toward the end of 1861 by the completion of the transcontinental telegraph. Although most mail is carried today by truck, specialized air-express services that promise overnight delivery are quite popular in the

United States. Automated physical delivery within a building through the use of pneumatic tubes was very popular in the nineteenth century, but the lack of a way to interconnect such systems to create a national service doomed this system to ultimate failure. (A possible business opportunity might be in the area of automated physical delivery, not only of letters, but also of small packages containing various small goods.)

As a form of communication, writing is long lasting. In a personal letter, the written word can be very intimate. People tend to express intimacies in a love letter that they would never express face-to-face. The letter takes time and thought to compose, and letter writing is believed to be a lost art because of the widespread use of instantaneous communication over electrical media, such as the telephone and e-mail.

BULLETIN BOARDS

Much interpersonal communication is of an intimate one-on-one nature. However, some interpersonal communication involves the transmission of a message from one person to a group of people. The classified advertisement section of a newspaper contains a large number of short messages intended to attract the attention of an interested party, such as someone searching for a job or a used automobile. These classified ads are delivered in a newspaper that is "broadcast" to a very large audience. The bulletin board is a way of pinpointing short messages for a much smaller audience.

The bulletin board is set up in a public place, and messages are attached to it. Sometimes the message is intended for a single person and might be inserted in an envelope and posted on the board—a method still used at conference meetings. Other times the message is intended for anyone interested enough to read it. Supermarkets frequently have bulletin boards where people post general messages, such as a car for sale or a babysitter wanted.

We shall see in a later chapter that one popular use of computers is to post and obtain messages from electronic bulletin boards and chat services.

TELEGRAPHY

In 1794, the Frenchman Claude Chappe built an optical two-arm semaphore system so that messages could be relayed from one hilltop station to another. The various positions of the two arms and the beam of the semaphore represented and encoded alphabetic letters and symbols. Chappe used the name *telegraph* to describe the system. It relied on the use of telescopes to see the position of each semaphore along the route. Obviously, this system did not work on a foggy day. It also was extremely slow, since the messages had to be relayed from one semaphore station to another. The solution was a telegraph system that used electricity to transmit instantly the encoding of the alphabetic letters and symbols—the electric telegraph—investigated and constructed by many inventors in the first half of the 1800s.

In 1816, Francis Ronalds in Great Britain developed an electromechanical telegraph system consisting of disks and pointers that worked over a single wire. In 1826, an American, Harrison Gray Dyer, invented an electrochemical telegraph system that generated bubbles at electrodes at the receiver. In 1831, Joseph Henry began experiments in New York with an electromagnetic telegraph system using an electric sounder as a receiver. A two-wire telegraph system using a galvanoscope-mirror detector was constructed in Germany in 1833 by Carl Friedrich Gauss and Wilhelm Eduard Weber. Samuel F. B. Morse and Alfred Vail demonstrated the dot-dash code in 1837 and installed a telegraph system between Baltimore and Washington in 1844. The British inventors William Fothergill Cooke and Sir Charles Wheatstone put the first telegraph system in England into service in 1839.

The serious problem with telegraphy was that Morse code had to be learned; thus trained telegraph operators were needed to encode and decode messages. Decoded messages were delivered physically at the destination, which precluded instantaneous interaction between communicators. Telegraphy was not an efficient means of communication for the general public. Today, the use of computers for e-mail is basically a return to the telegraphy of the mid-1800s, but is practicable on a far wider scale since there is no need to learn a complex code.

TELETYPEWRITER SERVICES

In 1846, a somewhat crude printing telegraph using a keyboard was invented in the United States by Royal E. House. This was followed in 1855 by the invention of a more practical printing telegraph using a keyboard—the teletypewriter or teleprinter—by the Anglo-American David Edward Hughes. The Hughes printing telegraph system sent a single dash per revolution to synchronize the sending and printing type-wheels. In 1872, the Frenchman Jean-Maurice-Emile Baudot invented a five-level code to indicate letters of the alphabet. However, the transmitting teletypewriter still had to be synchronized with the receiving teletypewriter using Hughes's method. An improved solution to the synchronization problem was the addition of a start bit and a stop bit to the five-level Baudot code. This innovation was used in the United States by Charles Krum in 1907, and Edward E. Kleinschmidt received a patent in 1915 for a start-stop teleprinter using the five-level Baudot code.

In 1917, AT&T introduced a teletypewriter service that interconnected terminals over private lines. The service was used mostly by newspapers and news-gathering organizations to send news reports. A switched teletypewriter exchange service, called TWX, was introduced by AT&T in 1931. In 1962, TWX was modified to operate on an automatic dial-up basis. TWX used either a conventional telephone circuit or a separate TWX network. A teletypewriter service, called TELEX, using the telephone network was introduced in Europe in the early 1930s and became international in the mid-1930s. In 1986, TELEX had 1.7 million subscribers in 207 countries. All these teletypewriter services operated at the relatively slow rate of sixty to one hundred words per minute. Their advantage was that a printed record of the message was received at the destination.

The teletypewriter eliminated the need to learn Morse code. The only required skill was the ability to operate an alphanumeric keyboard. However, special keyboards and printers, or other display devices, meant that this type of textual communication was costly and only available for businesses.

ELECTRONIC MAIL

Computers can communicate over the telephone network through the use of electronic devices called *modems* (short for *modulator-demodulator*). The computer can be used to compose an electronic letter or message that can then be sent over the telephone network to a recipient at another distant computer. Specialized data networks, such as the Internet, are used to carry the communication across continents and around the planet. Messages are stored at computerized databases for later retrieval.

This type of electronic, computerized communication of textual messages is known as *electronic mail*, or *e-mail*. The sender types a message with a keyboard and enters the computerized address of the recipient. The message is then sent over the Internet and is received and read on a visual display or is printed at the recipient's computer. The message can be addressed to a single recipient or sent to a number of people. E-mail is known as a form of computer-mediated communication. Sometimes, a group of people all working together on the same project use e-mail to keep in contact and to exchange views and opinions. The computer programs that facilitate this type of communication are called *groupware*. This group use of e-mail is sometimes called *computer conferencing*.

E-mail is enthusiastically used by many people. These people speak of the "thrill" and "magic" in "zapping" a message to another person. In many cases a person who would normally not write a letter does send an e-mail in response to another e-mail. Perhaps writing a letter is perceived as being too difficult and formal. There is a sense of immediacy with e-mail that is not matched by the conventional letter. However, facsimile also shares this sense of immediacy. While there still is the need to compose and write the fax letter, I have observed that people are willing to handwrite a short reply to a fax.

Two computers can be connected together over the Internet for real-time two-way communication at rates of 20 to 160 words per minute, depending upon how fast the user can type. The text message typed by one person is seen instantly by the other person—a service known as *instant messaging*.

The tremendous growth and acceptance of the Internet has greatly benefited e-mail, which is routinely used both at work and at home. In most cases it is easy to guess the e-mail address of most people, and friendly software makes its use easy and routine. But some people are bombarded by tremendous numbers of e-mail messages—some wanted, but many unwanted—all demanding immediate attention and response. Such e-mail communication can sometimes become too easy, leading to overuse and abuse. My solution is to be very reluctant to use it—except in the rarest cases and, even then, I try to keep my e-mail address private to a few trusted friends and colleagues.

THE INTERNET

The Internet achieved phenomenal growth during the second half of the 1990s. But the basic idea of packet switching of data, which forms one major aspect of the Internet, goes all the way back to the ARPANET, which initially became operational in the late 1960s.

What has made the Internet so successful today is the user-friendly interface, called the *World Wide Web*. This interface uses links, accessible through the use of the hypertext markup language (HTML) invented in 1989 by Tim

Berners-Lee, who was then working at the CERN nuclear physics laboratory in Switzerland. The first search engine to cruise the Web to catalogue all the information accessible over the Web was developed in 1993 by Marc Andreesen, while a graduate student at the University of Illinois.

One major use of the Internet is e-mail, discussed above. Another major use of the Internet is the access of information stored in many computerized databases distributed around the world. An Internet user can check weather forecasts and even look at satellite weather images to make one's own forecasts. Information about the financial performance of companies can be accessed. It is as if one has access to all the information that used to be stored only in file cabinets. It is possible to search for all sorts of goods and then order them over the Internet—but they nearly all still need to be delivered physically.

PHYSICAL DELIVERY

In our enthusiasm for the electronic delivery of various media, we often forget the importance of the physical delivery of a physical product. Goods might be ordered instantaneously by electronic media, but the physical product still needs to be delivered physically.

In many large cities, messenger services are very popular. Pedestrians in New York City have been nearly mowed down by messengers on bicycles zipping through traffic. In some cities, messengers use motorcycles to carry small parcels from one part of town to another—for only a few dollars.

Could technology be used to automate the physical delivery of small parcels within cities? Pneumatic tubes were used years ago to convey parcels from one portion of a building to another. Automated mail carts are in use in some office buildings. Could these local systems be linked somehow so that a small parcel could be sped from one part of the city to another?

The Internet is displacing the physical delivery of software. Computer programs and updates to computer software are routinely downloaded over the Internet. Recorded audio, particularly pop music, is being downloaded over the Internet, reducing the sales of such physical recordings as cassettes and CDs. Will video also be distributed over the Internet rather than physically?

REFERENCES
Breeden, Robert L., ed. *Those Inventive Americans*. Washington, D.C.: National
   Geographic Society, 1971.

Chappell, Warren. *A Short History of the Printed Word.* New York: Alfred A. Knopf, 1970.

Davies, W. V. *Egyptian Hieroglyphs.* Berkeley, Calif.: University of California Press/ British Museum, 1987.

Jean, Georges. *Writing: The Story of Alphabets and Scripts.* Translated by Jenny Oates. New York: Harry N. Abrams, 1992.

Robinson, Andrew. *The Story of Writing.* New York: Thames and Hudson, 1995.

Walsh, Len. *Read Japanese Today.* Tokyo: Charles E. Tuttle, 1969.

CHRONOLOGY

TELEGRAPH CHRONOLOGY

1819	Oersted discovery of electromagnetism.
1832	Samuel Finley Breese Morse obtains inspiration for telegraph from Dr. Charles T. Jackson while sailing from France to New York.
1837	Patent to Sir Charles Wheatstone (with W. Fothergill Cooke) for moving-needle system for sending letters.
1837	Agreement signed between Morse and Alfred Vail to construct model of telegraph. Morse to get all credit and patents.
1837	October 6—Morse files caveat at Patent Office.
1838	January 6—Machine finally completed by Vail, using dots/dashes.
1840	Patent issued to Morse.
1843	U.S. appropriates $30,000 to build telegraph line between Washington and Baltimore. Opened May 24.
1858	First transatlantic cable, but failed after a month.
1866	Transatlantic cable completed.

3

The World of Audio

Audio media encompass the recording and reproduction of sound, primarily music and speech. The old-fashioned phonograph with its hand crank and acoustic horn has evolved into today's electronic stereo system, with digital audio capable of wide dynamic and frequency ranges. The 78 rpm (revolutions per minute) phonograph record of the past has evolved into today's smaller-diameter compact disc. Along the way, the long-playing 33⅓ rpm disc appeared and reigned supreme for nearly half a century. Prerecorded cassettes are also available. These audio media are all mass reproduced and are delivered physically to the consumer.

The world of audio media also includes speech and music delivered over the air by broadcast radio. AM radio, used principally for speech, is of lower technical quality than FM radio, used mostly for music of all kinds. Although radio is mostly an entertainment medium, it is also an excellent source of news and other timely information. Many people hear first of important news events on the radio.

Audio media are listened to in the home, at work, in the automobile, and on the move. Most serious listening to recorded music probably takes place in the home using compact discs and cassettes. Many Americans spend much time in their automobiles commuting to and from work, listening to the radio, recorded cassettes, and compact discs. Many mass transit riders and exercisers use portable CD machines, and digital music units, such as the Apple iPod player, are becoming increasingly popular.

An interesting cross-combination of media has occurred recently. Complete or abridged books are recorded onto audiocassettes or compact discs and sold in bookstores. Commuters play the cassettes or discs in cars driving to and from work and also on long trips. This is an example of how the content of books—usually distributed through the medium of print on paper—can be transformed into an electronic recorded medium.

The physical delivery of mail is quite slow, even though most overnight air delivery services promise delivery the next morning within the United States. E-mail is instantaneous, requiring some expertise and a computer terminal to use it. The telephone requires no expertise beyond the ability to speak, is instantaneous, and today can go everywhere as the wireless cell phone. It is no wonder that it continues to be such an important component of the information age for instantaneous interpersonal telecommunication over distance.

THE PHONOGRAPH

The hand-cranked phonograph was invented by Thomas Alva Edison in 1877 and patented in 1888. Edison's phonograph used cylinders and a vertical, hill-and-dale method of recording. The flat disc and lateral, side-to-side recording was invented in 1887 by Emile Berliner, a German immigrant to the United States. A mechanical system of recording and reproduction was used with these early phonograph machines. Electric recording was perfected in 1924 by engineers at Bell Laboratories, and the speed of 78 rpm became standardized in 1925. The electric reproduction of sound was introduced a few years later. The 78 rpm speed was based on synchronizing the number of cranks per minute to the human heartbeat of about sixty to ninety beats per minute.

The plastic long-playing (LP) disc turning at 33⅓ rpm was invented by the Hungarian-born Peter Goldmark when he was working at CBS in the United States. Goldmark's LP disc, first demonstrated in 1948, had a diameter of twelve inches, like the older 78 rpm disc. But since the LP disc turned at a much slower rate and also had much narrower spaces between grooves, the LP disc had a much longer playing time. The LP also had a wider frequency range with less distortion and ushered in the dawn of high-fidelity audio. RCA countered with the introduction in 1949 of the smaller-diameter (seven-inch) 45 rpm disc. Both discs survived for decades, with popular single pieces offered on the 45 disc and classical music and collections (albums) of popular pieces offered on the LP disc.

The basic concepts needed for the stereo LP record were invented in the late 1950s by engineers at the Westrex Company, owned by AT&T. In 1958, the stereophonic LP record was introduced; the signal for each stereo channel was recorded on each wall of the groove. Stereophonic audio systems with two separate channels and loudspeakers added a depth and realism to recorded sound that was quickly accepted by consumers. Within five years, the old monophonic LP was replaced by the stereo LP. Engineers at Columbia Records had improved on the stereo LP invention by making the record compatible with older single-channel monophonic systems also.

Columbia introduced the four-channel quadraphonic disc in the early 1970s, but it met with poor consumer acceptance and was withdrawn. The quadraphonic system required four loudspeakers, and this was probably too complex and costly for the scarcely noticeable improvement in the sound. High-end large-screen television sets that attempt to recreate the movie theater experience in the home have created a new market for four-channel surround sound.

The digital audio compact disc (CD) was introduced in the early 1980s, and by the end of that decade, the black vinyl LP was no longer available for classical music. The CD offered a considerable improvement in audio quality, coupled with ease of handling and more durability than the LP. The 1990s saw the disappearance of the LP for all types of music.

Phonograph records, compact discs, and cassettes all involve mechanics in the form of rotating and moving media, either discs or tape. The MP3 and other formats compress the digital audio signal and reproduce it on small portable players. With many of the players, there are no mechanics. Compressed audio is truly an audio chip, heralding the end of mechanical sound storage!

AUDIO RECORDING

In 1888, Oberlin Smith, working in New Jersey, wrote an article in a magazine in the United States that proposed a recording and reproducing system using magnetization of a long wire. In 1898, the Dane Valdemar Poulsen invented a magnetic recording system using steel wire and took his invention to the production stage. The use of thin, flexible magnetic tape for recording sound was patented in 1928 by the German Fritz Pfleumer. The tape was stored on reels. Reel-to-reel tape recorders were used primarily by professionals. Two-channel, stereophonic tape recording was invented in 1946.

Although RCA had earlier invented a tape cartridge the size of a paper-back book, home use of audio recorders did not really take hold until the early 1960s when engineers at Philips Electronics developed the small audio-cassette. A larger eight-track cassette appeared at about the same time and was proposed for use in automobiles, but in the end, the Philips cassette conquered the market. Today, many people have cassette players in their automobiles and listen to prerecorded cassettes, although the digital compact disc is replacing cassettes.

Video recorders were first used in the late 1970s to record professional performances of music for which the audio signals had been converted to a digital format. The digital format offered a wider range of frequencies, much less distortion, a larger dynamic range, and much less noise. Engineers at Philips, with assistance from engineers at Sony, developed the compact disc (CD) and introduced it to the marketplace in 1983. The 4¾-inch-diameter CD stores digital information and is played by a laser beam.

A small cassette has been developed so that digital audio can be recorded on its tape in the home. Techniques for recording digital audio directly onto a CD are also available. However, there are doubts about whether most consumers really have a need for the high quality offered by digital recording.

RECORDED-AUDIO CONTENT

The world of recorded music seems to fall into two major categories, depending on the content of the medium: classical and popular/rock. Nearly all classical recordings are presently on the CD format; the old 33⅓ LP record is obsolete. Most popular and rock music recordings have also shifted to the CD format.

The old 45 rpm single was used mostly for popular/rock music and was purchased mostly by teenagers and youngsters. A CD with a three-inch diameter was introduced as a possible replacement for the 45, but its cost was too high for the market. The three-inch CD could hold only about fifteen minutes of music, which was far too short for most major classical pieces. Thus, the three-inch CD has virtually disappeared from the market in the United States. The audiocassette is used mostly by people on the move with their Walkman players and in their automobiles. A short cassette that holds only about ten minutes of music was introduced for pop/rock singles and was quite successful. The cassette single (cassingle) sold for a few dollars, which undoubtedly accounted for its success as a replacement for the 45 single.

In the area of popular music, an interesting innovation was the custom audiocassette marketed by Personics. The customer was able to choose a number of individual pieces of music, and they were recorded on a cassette at the store for purchase by the customer. But the system met with low consumer acceptance and disappeared from the market.

Media, such as cassettes and CDs, can also record human speech. Spoken drama used to be very popular on radio before the advent of TV. The audiobook, discussed earlier, is today's equivalent to radio drama and is primarily listened to in the automobile during the daily commute to work. Audiocassettes have been used as an educational tool to help learn a foreign language, but the compact disc with its much greater ease of access is a better medium for educational audio.

HIGH FIDELITY

Edison's hand-cranked phonograph with its poor sound quality has evolved over the last hundred years to today's high-fidelity electronic stereo system. The development of modern consumer electronics that followed World War II was a major factor in the growth of the hi-fi industry. Yesterday's vacuum-tube amplifiers were bulky and weighty affairs suffering from much noise and hum. Today's transistorized amplifiers offer higher quality and more output power. The loudspeakers of the past were very large and bulky. Much better sound quality is produced by the much smaller bookcase-sized loudspeakers of today.

In its early days, high-fidelity systems consisted of a single, monophonic channel. Today's high-fidelity systems are two-channel, stereophonic systems offering a sense of spaciousness and depth.

RADIO

Radio waves were first discovered by the American physicist Joseph Henry in 1842. The mathematical principles of radio waves were formulated in 1864 by the Scottish physicist James Clerk Maxwell. In 1875, Thomas Alva Edison observed the effects of radio waves but did not pursue their practical use. The Anglo-American David Edward Hughes built a crude radio transmitter and receiver in 1879 but likewise failed to pursue its practical use. The German physicist Heinrich Hertz demonstrated radio waves in 1888 and is generally credited with their discovery.

In 1894 the Englishman Oliver Lodge built a sensitive radio receiver using the coherer radio-wave detector invented in 1890 by the Frenchman Edouard Branly. The Italian Guglielmo Marconi transmitted the first radio waves across the Atlantic in 1901. Croatian immigrant to the United States Nikola Tesla performed experiments and demonstrations of radio broadcasting as early as 1893 and realized the potential of radio waves for communication. During these early years, radio was used as a form of wireless telegraphy for communication. The use of radio for broadcasting speech and music to a large audience came later.

The practical use of radio was made possible by the invention of the diode in 1904 by John Ambrose Fleming in Great Britain. The invention of the triode in 1906 by the American Lee De Forest made amplification possible, and in 1907 De Forest performed experiments in the use of radio to broadcast music. In 1906, the Canadian Reginald Aubrey Fessenden was the first to use radio with modulation of a high-frequency, pure-tone carrier wave to broadcast music and speech. The invention of the superheterodyne principle in 1918 by Edwin H. Armstrong provided a practical way to produce good-quality radio receivers.

The first commercial radio station was the Westinghouse station, KDKA, which began broadcasting in 1920 in Pennsylvania. It was preceded by the experimental radio station 8XK, started by Westinghouse employee Frank Conrad. In 1922, the AT&T radio station WEAF in New York City was the first station to accept advertising. In 1922, only 0.2 percent of households in the United States owned a radio receiver. Ten years later, 60 percent of households owned radio receivers. Clearly, radio was a very popular form of mass entertainment.

Early radio stations used the principle of amplitude modulation (AM) to broadcast the radio signal. AM broadcast radio operates in a frequency band from 535 to 1605 kHz. Each radio station occupies a 10 kHz band of frequencies. The audio signal can have no frequencies higher than 5 kHz, which, though suitable for speech, is less acceptable for music. AM radio suffers from noise as well.

In 1933 Edwin H. Armstrong was the first to recognize that wideband frequency modulation offered considerable improvement in noise reduction over AM. FM broadcast radio began in 1939 but was dealt a setback in 1948, when the radio band of frequencies was moved to a higher band. This move by the FCC forced listeners to purchase new radios to receive the new band. FM radio stations operate in a range of 88 to 108 MHz, and each station occupies a band of frequencies that is 200 kHz wide. FM radio carries an audio signal with a maximum frequency of 15 kHz, which is very acceptable for high-fidelity reproduction. Also, in 1961 FM radio broadcast stereophonic audio using a multiplex technique that retained compatibility with conventional monophonic receivers. By 1967, nearly all high-fidelity FM radio tuners were stereo. These factors meshed well with the rise of consumer acceptance of high fidelity and led to considerable growth in FM radio. In 1989, although there were slightly more AM radio stations than FM stations, the FM audience was nearly three times the AM audience.

INTERNET AUDIO

The telephone network could have been used to obtain access to radio programs and to music, but the cost of doing so on a wide scale would have been prohibitive. It was much less costly to broadcast the same program to many listeners over radio and to distribute music over prerecorded media, such as records, tapes, and CDs.

Today, the Internet is being used to access radio programs to listen to music and other programs. Real-time listening is accomplished over the Internet through a technique known as *audio streaming*. Music can be transmitted over the Internet and listened to later—a technique known as *downloading*.

The same economic and technological issues exist that would have been encountered had the telephone network been used for broadcasting. To conserve bandwidth with streaming and downloading, the audio is compressed, which usually compromises quality somewhat, but it is still more than acceptable. One compression scheme used for music is called *MP3*.

So many people were downloading music on the Internet that issues over copyright created serious concerns about this use—some would claim abuse—of the Internet.

SATELLITE RADIO

Communication satellites located in geostationary orbits above the equator are able to transmit signals that can cover large geographic areas. The signals are sent from Earth to the satellite and then are rebroadcast from the satellite back to Earth. Such technology has been used for years to send television signals across the planet for television networks and more recently to homes. This technology is known as direct broadcast satellite (DBS) TV.

Satellites are also now being used to send broadcast audio. However, the user must purchase a special radio receiver and must also subscribe to a monthly service to decode the received signals. But since conventional radio is free, the future success of such a paid service is unclear.

TELEPHONY

The telephone is generally acknowledged to have been invented by the Scottish-Canadian Alexander Graham Bell working in Boston in 1876. However, the American inventor Elisha Gray appears to have also invented key principles of telephony at the same time, and the German Philip Reis had built a telephone system as early as 1861. Regardless of who actually invented the telephone, it was Theodore N. Vail who founded the Bell System and who realized the importance of making telephone service affordable to as many people as possible. Bell and Vail had the vision of a national network interconnecting telephones everywhere.

What makes the telephone so useful is its ease of use. No special skills are necessary to speak on the telephone, and it accurately conveys the nuances and intimacies of human speech. And because telephoning is voice-only communication, in some circumstances it might enable closer and more intimate communication than face-to-face interaction. Telephonic communication is a wonderful invention!

The telephone network is a switched network that connects one telephone to any other telephone. The first automated switching system was invented by Almon B. Strowger in 1892. Automated switching eventually displaced human operators and helped make telephone service universally affordable. Today's telephone network, or public switched network, extends all over the globe. Telephone signals are carried over copper wire, microwave radio, and optical fiber. The signals are converted to digital form and are switched by computer-controlled switching systems. The public switched network is capable of carrying signals other than voice and hence is a flexible, ubiquitous resource of considerable utility.

In the early days of telephone service, a number of parties were connected to the same telephone line—a form of service known as *party-line service.*

Etiquette barred one from listening to other people's conversations. Today, nearly all telephone service is private-line service. It is interesting, though, that "new" chat lines have evolved for dating and other purposes in which the user dials a special number and is then connected to a number of other persons. These chat-line services are a way to use the telephone to reach a small number of other people simultaneously in a fashion also somewhat similar to citizens band radio.

MOBILE TELECOMMUNICATION: CELL PHONES

The conventional telephone is a point-to-point form of interpersonal telecommunication conducted over copper wires. However, nowadays most people are on the move at work and at play. This has created a need for two-way mobile telecommunication, which must be conducted over radio as opposed to over wires. Since the automobile is the most popular form of personal transportation, mobile radio telecommunication with automobiles was developed.

Mobile radio telecommunication is not new, but the systems of the past were very limited in capacity and were quite costly. The solution was the invention of the cellular concept by engineers at Bell Labs. Cellular mobile telephone service was finally introduced commercially in the United States in 1983 after a decade of regulatory delay by the Federal Communications Commission and has grown tremendously since then. The service was initially intended for automobiles, but very small portable cellular telephones now make mobile wireless service possible anywhere.

Cellular service allows connection to the public switched network from an automobile or almost anywhere the cellular telephone may be. Although originally intended for two-way voice telecommunication, cellular is now even used for facsimile transmission by business people who are always on the move and who in essence work out of their automobiles.

Another form of wireless telephony is the cordless telephone that has been available for many years. Cordless telephones work within a home or office and use two-way radio from the cordless handset to a unit that connects to the telephone line. Cordless telephones typically work only over a very small distance.

In the 1960s, a portion of the radio spectrum was made available for low-powered two-way radio telecommunication over a few dozen channels. This service was called citizens band radio, or CB. Many CB radios were installed in automobiles and were used to chat during long trips and to find out about police radar traps along highways. Truckers used CB radio for similar purposes. CB radio did not connect to the telephone network and thus was limited in value. Furthermore, simultaneous two-way communication was not possible, and the user had to pause to allow the other person to speak, just as with the push-to-talk feature of airplane radio. CB radio was not private, and anyone could listen in and join a conversation. This "chat" feature of CB radio would later find extension to the telephone network and "new" chat services that allow a number of people to telephone a phone number and all talk together. Two-way radios are used to keep in contact when shopping at the mall or when hiking in the woods.

Telephone service was first made available in many commercial airplanes using GTE's Airfone service. The user inserts a credit card in a unit similar to a pay telephone and removes a portable handset. The actual call can then be made from anywhere inside the airplane. The connection is by two-way radio from the airplane to one of a number of strategically located ground stations, and the final connection is made over the public switched telephone network.

Pagers are another way of reaching people who are constantly on the move. Old-style pagers made a beeping sound when someone was being paged. The person paged then had to telephone an exchange to obtain the number of the person to call. Newer pagers have a small display that shows the number of the calling person and even a short text message.

So great is the need perceived to be to reach some people who are always on the move that an ultimate service might be to assign a universal personal number to everyone that follows us wherever we may be. Someone trying to reach us could simply dial that number and we would be called at home, at work, in the car, at the restaurant, or at the hotel. However, I wonder how many people really want to be that reachable all the time.

CHAT LINES

In many large cities, it seems that nearly all of the commercials on late-night television are for various chat-line services. These services enable a group of people to speak together on telephones or to leave messages for other callers. Conceptually, today's chat lines are akin to yesterday's party-line telephone service. However, it was considered impolite to listen in to other people's conversations back then. Today's chat lines are more like CB radio in which a number of people listen and speak together.

Bulletin board services allow computer users to type messages to each other over the Internet. They are a form of chat-line service using text.

REFERENCES

Douglas, Susan J. *Inventing American Broadcasting: 1899–1922*. Baltimore, Md.: Johns Hopkins University Press, 1987.

Isom, Warren Rex, ed. "The Phonograph and Sound Recording after One-Hundred Years: Centennial Issue." *Journal of the Audio Engineering Society* 25, no. 10/11 (October/November 1977).

Lewis, Tom. *Empire of the Air: The Men Who Made Radio*. New York: Edward Burlingame Books, 1991.

Mackay, James. *Alexander Graham Bell: A Life*. New York: John Wiley & Sons, 1997.

RADIO CHRONOLOGY

1860s	American dentist Mahlon Loomis uses flying kite with a long wire dangling from it and detects impulses on another kite eighteen miles away.
1864	James Clerk Maxwell formulates theory of electromagnetic waves.
1865	Maxwell publishes paper on mathematical theory of electromagnetic waves.
1875	Thomas Alva Edison observes radio sparking phenomenon, calls it an "etheric force" but does not pursue.
1883	Edison discovers unidirectional current flow in lamp tube.
1888	Heinrich Rudolph Hertz produces and detects radio waves with spark gaps.
1893	Nikola Tesla demonstrates tuned spark-gap transmitter and receiver. Results widely described and published.
1894	Oliver Lodge in England develops coherer as wave detector and demonstrates Hertzian waves.
1896	Guglielmo Marconi arrives in Great Britain to develop radio.
1897	Marconi radio patent.
1898	Radio patent granted to Tesla.
1899	October 4—International Yacht Races in New York harbor off Sandy Hook covered by Marconi's wireless telegraph.
1900	Tesla article describes vision of radio broadcasting to masses.
1901	Marconi sends letter "S" across Atlantic.
1902	December 21—Marconi sends full message across Atlantic.
1904	J. Ambrose Fleming creates improved diode valve.
1906	"Cat's whisker" crystal detector invented by H. H. Dunwoody and G. W. Pickard.

1906	Lee De Forest describes "audion" tube at professional AIEE meeting in New York City.
1906	December 24—Reginald Aubrey Fessenden conducts experiment using continuous waves to carry human voice, broadcast from Massachusetts.
1909	Marconi shares Nobel Prize in Physics with Karl Ferdinand Braun.
1912	Edwin Howard Armstrong discovers regenerative and oscillatory feedback circuits.
1912	*Radio Act of 1912* passed—licenses required for radio.
1913	Armstrong files for patents on regenerative and oscillatory feedback circuits, and demonstrates regenerative circuit to Marconi people, including David Sarnoff.
1914	De Forest narrowly misses jail for mail fraud over radio stock promotion.
1917	United States enters World War I and takes over radio as allowed by *Radio Act of 1912*.
1918	Armstrong invents superheterodyne circuit and applies for patent.
1919	Radio Corporation of America created by GE, Westinghouse, and AT&T.
1920	Frank Conrad of Westinghouse broadcasts music to hams from his garage near Pittsburgh, and local department store sells Westinghouse radios.
1922	The radio boom begins.
1933	Wideband FM patents issued to Armstrong.
1943	United States Supreme Court rules that Tesla's fundamental radio patents anticipated Marconi and all others.
1943	FM stations start to appear all over.

TELEPHONE CHRONOLOGY

1860	M. Reiss in Friedrichsdorf builds tuned apparatus, but speech is not intelligible.
1876	February 14—Alexander Graham Bell files for patent. Elisha Gray files caveat.
1876	March 10—Bell and Thomas A. Watson obtain first working telephone.
1878	August 1—Watson files for patent on bell ringer.
1880	Bell invents photophone using light to carry telephone signals.
1881	John J. Carty invents second metallic wire for local loop.
1881	William Wheeler (American) granted patent for light pipes.
1886	Thomas Alva Edison invents carbon-granule microphone.
1887	British physicist Charles Vernon Boys describes use of thin glass fibers to carry light.
1892	First automated switching system installed—invented by Almon B. Strowger—used rotary dialer at telephone.
1899	Loading coil invented by Professor Michael I. Pupin—enabled long lines.
1938	First crossbar switching system installed for use in Bell System.
1946	First coaxial cable across United States for long-distance telephony.
1950	First use of microwave radio across United States for telephone service—used FM.
1959	AT&T's first transatlantic coaxial cable system placed in service carrying 72 voice circuits.
1962	Telstar I launched.

1962	T1 digital system first used for interoffice trunking.
1963	Touchtone dialing initiated.
1963	Hughes's Snycom II launched for geosynchronous, intercontinental communication.
1965	First computer-controlled switching system, No. 1 ESS, installed in Bell system.
1970	AT&T introduces picturephone service.
1976	First digital switching system, No. 4 ESS, installed for use by AT&T.
1979	AT&T's first optical fiber system, FT3, introduced.
1983	First commercial cellular service offered in United States in Chicago.
1984	AT&T breakup with creation of seven "Baby Bells."

Still and Moving Images

An image or a picture is pleasing and entertaining—and moving pictures on a screen at the movie theater are even better. But perhaps better yet is bringing moving images directly into the home through the wonders of television.

This chapter describes various broadcast media for both still and moving images. The chapter includes a description of teletext, which is a broadcast medium for delivering text and graphic images to the home. While teletext might have been included in the previous chapter on print media, it is also included here since it displays images on the home TV set.

The telephone network is used mostly for human speech. However, it is a switched network that can also convey other types of signals, such as stationary and moving images. Facsimile and the picturephone, which both use switched networks, are described at the end of this chapter.

PHOTOGRAPHY

The basic principles of photography were described in a paper given in 1802 by the Englishman Thomas Wedgwood. Another Englishman, Henry Fox Talbot, invented the negative process in 1839 and was awarded a patent in 1841. The first photograph of a scene of nature was made in 1826 using the camera obscura invented in France by Joseph-Nicéphone Niépce. Metal plates coated with silver iodide were first used in 1837 by another Frenchman, Louis-Jacques-Mandé Daguerre. Celluloid film was introduced in 1888 by

George Eastman in the United States. Color film was invented by Leopold D. Mannes and Leopold Godowsky, and was first marketed in 1935 by the Eastman Kodak Company.

A problem with conventional photography using a negative is that the film needs to be developed and then printed at a laboratory with the necessary chemicals and processes. The solution was the invention of instant photography by Edwin Land in 1943. The sale of instant cameras to the public started in 1948. Enhancements to instant photography included color and faster developing of the print.

An innovation, first developed in the mid-1980s by Sony, was electronic photography in which a camera produced an electronic image on a small computer disk or flat rectangular card. The information on the disk was displayed on a television receiver, or a special printer could make a print. The early consumer market for the electronic camera was negligible, but photojournalists used it and transmitted the electronic photos to their editorial offices over a communication satellite link or a phone line. Today's version of the electronic camera is the digital camera that interfaces with the home computer and its printer.

Realism in photography was enhanced through the use of color. A further enhancement is stereoscopy. The basic principle of stereoscopy (3-D) was invented in 1838 by the British scientist Sir Charles Wheatstone. The refracting type of stereoscope and the twin camera were invented by David Brewster in 1844. Although the stereoscope was once quite popular, it has become a rarity and today is found in very few homes.

MOTION PICTURES

The principle of creating the illusion of motion from a series of still images was first demonstrated in 1877 by Eadweard Muybridge, an English emigrant living in California. In 1888, William Dickson, working at Edison's laboratories, utilized long rolls of Eastman celluloid film for a series of photographs of a moving event. This film technique for moving images was patented in 1891, and the Edison kinetoscope was used to show peep shows to one person at a time for five cents—the nickelodeon. In 1895, the French brothers Auguste and Louis Lumière invented a portable, hand-cranked camera and a movie projector, both operating at sixteen frames per second.

Early motion pictures were silent. Synchronized sound was added in 1927 based on inventions of the American Lee De Forest. The Technicolor three-color process was introduced in 1932 and was followed by the three-projector Cinerama process in 1952, and by the single-projector CinemaScope process with its special lens in 1953. Other enhancements of motion pictures that did not achieve much market acceptance were stereoscopic (3-D) movies and Smell-A-Vision.

For motion pictures, the still images are shown at a rate of twenty-four frames per second. Each frame is exposed twice on the screen through the use of a shutter. This is done to avoid flicker.

Home movies were promoted using narrower 16 mm and 8 mm film, but these movies never really achieved popularity with consumers. Small, portable video camera recorders (camcorders) seem to be more acceptable to consumers, perhaps because they can view the resulting video immediately on a standard TV set. Newer camcorders record the video signal digitally and can be connected to personal computers to edit and save the video.

TELEVISION

Television is a broadcast entertainment medium offering images in full motion along with high-quality audio. Television was introduced commercially in the United States in 1946, and by the end of the year, 0.02 percent of households had a TV set. Consumer acceptance was phenomenal, and by 1956, 72 percent of households had at least one TV set. Variety shows, news, movies, situation comedies, and talk shows are some of the types of programming offered over television.

The basic concepts used in television are very old: an electromechanical scanning disk was first used in 1884 by the German Paul Nipkow. Early pioneers in television were Charles Francis Jenkins, who demonstrated a system in 1923 in the United States, and John Logie Baird, who demonstrated a system in 1925 in Britain. The electronic camera tube was invented in 1933 by Vladimir K. Zworykin, a Russian immigrant to the United States working for RCA. A public demonstration of an all-electronic television system was given in 1928 by the American Philo T. Farnsworth.

The first government-approved broadcast of color television took place in 1950 using a field-sequential system invented by CBS. However, the field-sequential system was not compatible with the older black-and-white system.

Compatibility was achieved with the invention of the NTSC (National Television System Committee) system by RCA engineers, with the strong financial commitment of RCA's David Sarnoff. The NTSC system became the United States standard and broadcasts began in 1953. Since most consumers had only recently purchased a black-and-white TV set, the growth of color television was comparatively slow.

Television signals are broadcast into the home over the air using either the VHF (very high frequency) band or the UHF (ultra high frequency) band. The VHF bands used for television transmission extend from 54 MHz to 88 MHz and from 174 MHz to 216 MHz, and the UHF band extends from 470 MHz to 806 MHz. A total of twelve TV channels are available in the VHF band, and fifty-six channels are available in the UHF band.

The audio portion of television is transmitted separately from the video. Frequency modulation is used for the audio portion, and the quality of the audio signal is comparable to FM radio. In 1984, the quality was further improved when the FCC authorized multichannel stereophonic sound for television. Today many programs are broadcast in stereo. A stereo-compatible TV receiver and two loudspeakers are required to decode and hear the stereo audio signal.

Television frames are displayed at a rate of about thirty per second. Each frame breaks into two interlaced fields, one consisting of the odd-numbered scan lines and the other of the even-numbered scan lines. This is done to avoid flicker, in a fashion somewhat similar to the system used in motion pictures.

Television signals are also broadcast into homes over the coaxial cable of the CATV industry. As many as one hundred, or perhaps even more, TV channels can be broadcast over the coaxial cable. CATV began in 1958 as a way for a community to share a single large antenna to receive TV at a location distant from the broadcasting site. Thus, the term *CATV* originally stood for *community antenna TV*. Later, CATV was used in large cities to improve reception by avoiding ghosts. Today, *CATV* denotes *cable TV* and offers many more channels than are available with conventional VHF and UHF television.

Communication satellites located in geostationary orbits over the equator are also used to send television signals to homes. These signals are sent from Earth up to the satellites, which then retransmit them to Earth, covering a large area, or footprint. This form of satellite television is called direct broadcast satellite (DBS) TV and currently is subscribed to by about 15 percent of homes in the United States.

Conventional television in the United States has 525 scan lines. A higher-quality form of television called high-definition television (HDTV), offering over one thousand scan lines and a wider viewing display, is currently broadcast in digital form and is to be the new standard. Since the original 525-line standard was developed taking into account the resolution of human vision, a new 1,000-line standard might not offer a noticeable improvement in image resolution unless the display is very large or is viewed very closely.

Advanced television promises more programs in the spectrum space of a single conventional TV channel. These additional programs could be multiple camera shots of sporting events, the same program sent in a time-displaced manner, or many different programs.

VIDEO RECORDING

The earliest attempts at recording television signals were performed by the Scotsman John Logie Baird in 1927. He recorded the television signals on 78 rpm discs. The use of magnetic tape for recording television signals was perfected by engineers at Ampex in the United States, and their video recorder was introduced in 1956 for use in the TV studio. The Ampex machine used reels to hold the tape. In 1969, Sony introduced the U-Matic video recorder, which used cassettes. It was intended for home use, but because of its high cost, it was used mostly by professionals.

The home video recorder was introduced in 1976 by Sony and used tape in a cassette. Sony's Betamax format was soon followed by the VHS format developed by Sony's competitors. The home VCR (videocassette recorder) has improved in quality, and the cassette has shrunk in size for use in handheld portable video cameras. A whole new industry has developed solely to rent prerecorded videos of movies to consumers. Many consumers use their VCRs to record TV shows off the air for later viewing at a more convenient time.

From time to time, prerecorded videodiscs twelve inches in diameter have been developed and introduced into the marketplace. Videodisc systems were invented in 1966 by the Telefunken Corporation and in 1969 by RCA. In 1981, RCA introduced its SelectaVision videodisc system. It was poorly received by consumers and was withdrawn in 1984. A similar fate was met by optical videodiscs, developed by the Philips Corporation, which were played by a laser beam. The twelve-inch laser videodisc was reintroduced in the early 1990s, but again was poorly accepted by consumers.

A small-diameter digital video disc (the DVD) was introduced in the late 1990s. Consumers adopted it very quickly, and DVDs are now available in video rental stores. A recordable form of DVD has been developed.

RECORDED-VIDEO CONTENT

The home videocassette recorder (VCR) can be used to record anything that is broadcast over television. The VCR can also be used to play prerecorded tapes purchased or rented from video stores. Movies are the prime content of videotapes.

CATV has learned to copy radio in content. Individual radio stations specialize in content; for example, a news station, a talk station, or a rock station. CATV channels do the same—CNN for news, TNT for drama, rock stations for rock video, and so forth. The rock video has spilled over to videocassettes. There seems to be a market for watching video while listening to rock.

TELETEXT

Teletext is a broadcast general-interest information service. The user presses a number on the remote control that is assigned to the specific topic being sought. The information is then displayed on the screen of the home television receiver as a page of text with some graphics. A full page of text is usually about twenty-four rows of forty characters each. All the pages in the database of information are sent repetitively in a round-robin fashion. Typically the whole database consists of a few hundred pages of information, and this entire database is sent in about thirty seconds. Thus an individual page can be retrieved in about fifteen seconds on the average. The pages of information are encoded and inserted in the nonvisible vertical retrace portion of the television signal and in that way are sent along with the normal television signal.

News, weather, sports scores, and financial reports are some of the timely information that is available with teletext. In a way, teletext is like radio except that the information is read on a screen and is available nearly instantly. Teletext offers instant access to timely, general-interest information. Teletext is free to the consumer, except for the extra cost of a teletext-equipped TV set. The cost of the computer and other equipment needed to insert the teletext information in the TV signal is very low.

Teletext was invented and first offered by the British in the early 1970s. The teletext service offered by the British Broadcasting Corporation is called Ceefax, and the Independent Broadcasting Authority's teletext service is called Oracle. In the mid-1980s, there were about one million teletext-equipped TV sets in use in Britain, and today all new TV sets sold in Britain are teletext equipped. Teletext is also available in most of Europe and Scandinavia.

Teletext uses technology known as a *frame grabber*. When the desired frame comes around, it is grabbed, stored, and displayed on the screen of the TV set. Such technology was developed in the early 1970s by the Mitre Corporation in an advanced cable television system called TICCIT for use in a planned community in Reston, Virginia. The National Bureau of Standards developed technology, called *closed-captioning*, for transmitting text during the vertical retrace interval of the TV signal as an aid for the hearing impaired. Teletext is a broader and more flexible successor to these early efforts.

FACSIMILE

Facsimile, or fax, is a way of sending a copy of material on paper over distance. The material on the paper is converted to an electrical signal that is then transmitted over the public switched telephone network. At its destination, the received signal is converted to hard copy on paper. The material on the paper can be text, a drawing, or even a photograph.

Facsimile is very old, and its basic principles were invented in 1842 by the Scotsman Alexander Bain. The drum recorder with its rotating cylinder was invented in 1848 by Frederick C. Bakewell in London. In 1902, the German Arthur Korn invented a facsimile system using a selenium photoelectric cell for transmitting photographs. The first wire photo was sent by facsimile from Cleveland to New York in 1924.

Modern facsimile machines are easy to use and are fast: a single page can be sent in about one minute. International standardization means that any fax machine can communicate with any other fax machine. The flexibility of being able to send anything on a piece of paper is a strong advantage of the fax. Because of time differences and language differences, facsimile is an efficient way to communicate across continents. Faxing has become so popular that some sandwich shops in large cities have a fax machine for noontime take-out orders. Personal computers are also used to send and to receive facsimile documents.

TELEWRITER

The telewriter, or telautograph, was invented around 1888 by Elisha Gray. The telewriter transmits an exact duplicate of a handwritten message or drawing as the handwriting takes place. Gray's early telewriters used mechanical linkages to sense the movement of the pen, which was then converted to electric signals for transmission over wire circuits, usually connecting the transmitter and receiver in the premises of a business. Modern telewriters use electronic sensing of the movement of the handwriting pen.

PICTUREPHONE

The telephone enables two people to speak with each other over great distances through the use of a switched network. The picturephone is an extension of the telephone to include moving images so that the conversant not only can speak and be heard but can also see and be seen. Advocates of the picturephone believe that the addition of the visual modality greatly enhances the value of interpersonal telecommunication by telephone.

In the late 1920s, engineers at Bell Telephone Laboratories conducted studies of the use of an electromechanical television system to send moving images of one person speaking live to another person at a distant location. These early studies evolved into the picturephone system, which was demonstrated at the New York World's Fair in 1964. AT&T interpreted the consumer response to the demonstration as being positive enough to justify full-scale development of a picturephone communication system. Picturephone service was introduced initially in 1970 in Pittsburgh, and service was extended to Chicago the following year. The consumer acceptance was very poor, and in 1972 AT&T in effect withdrew the service and entered a period of market study. The conclusion was that most consumers had little, if any, need to see the other person while speaking over the telephone. A need was expressed to exchange graphic information, however.

In the mid-1980s, small picturephone-like telephones costing about $400 each and working over regular telephone circuits were introduced. These devices produced a coarse image with blurred motion. Like AT&T's

picturephone, these products failed to excite consumer interest. In the early 1990s, AT&T introduced a videophone that worked over regular telephone lines, but it too failed in the marketplace.

The inescapable conclusion is that most people have no need to see the other person while speaking over the telephone. Perhaps the visual imagery somehow destroys the intimacy of telephonic communication, or perhaps it is too restrictive and is considered an invasion of personal privacy to be on camera. Even if the costs are decreased and if the quality is improved, I am convinced that the consumer reaction is so negative that there is no market now nor will there be in the future for picturephone communication.

TELECONFERENCING

Meetings between groups of people occur very frequently in most companies and industries. Travel from one corporate location to another to attend such meetings quite often wastes time and incurs much expense. Teleconferencing, also known as telemeeting, is the use of telecommunication to enable a group of people at one location to "meet" with a group of people at one or more other locations.

A wide variety of audio and video communication can be used for teleconferencing—ranging from simple audio-only to two-way full-motion video—as listed below:

- audio only
- audio + facsimile
- audio + interactive graphics
- one-way compressed video, with audio
- one-way full-motion video, with audio
- two-way compressed video, with audio
- two-way full-motion video, with audio

Clearly, audio-only teleconferencing is the least costly since only a simple telephone circuit is needed. The audio quality can be improved considerably if additional audio bandwidth is purchased from the telecommunication carrier. Visual material can be sent in advance of the meeting by air express or during the meeting by facsimile and projected simultaneously at both meeting sites. The need to draw images and have them be seen by the participants at both locations can be satisfied by the use of one-way and two-way interactive graphic systems that work over an additional telephone circuit.

Full-motion video is very costly in terms of bandwidth, since 4.5 MHz of analog bandwidth in each direction is required. Because there is little movement from video frame to video frame during a teleconference, the transmitted image can be compressed in bandwidth, although smearing will occur if considerable movement occurs. This trade-off is quite acceptable for most video teleconferences, and bit rates under 1 Mbps are acceptable for digital transmission.

The various modalities available for teleconferencing range from simple audio-only systems to costly, top-of-the-line, two-way full-motion video. Although it has been estimated that there is a very large market for video teleconferencing, the number of video systems in use is actually quite small.

Communication technology is not the determining factor in ensuring the use of teleconferencing. The type and purpose of the meeting is much more important. Research indicates that the regularly occurring, information-exchange meeting is the best candidate for teleconferencing. I estimate that only about 4 percent of all group meetings meet this requirement. This would explain the relatively low use of group teleconferencing.

Most teleconferencing involves a group of participants at each location. However, there are cases where one person wishes to interact with a group of people at a distant location. For example, a corporate executive who may wish to reach employees at one or many distant locations with the same message. One-way video is quite adequate for this situation, possibly augmented with two-way audio so that the people at the distant locations can ask questions. Video teleconferencing has been used for decades by some engineering schools to enable groups of students at remote locations to tele-attend class, thereby avoiding a wasteful commute.

CHRONOLOGY

TELEVISION CHRONOLOGY

1872	Joseph May (working in Ireland) notices that the resistance of selenium changes when exposed to light.
1883	Paul Nipkow (German) invents rotating disk to scan images and send them over wires.
1884	German patent issued for Nipkow disk.
1906	Max Diekmann (German) invents cathode ray tube (cold).
1907	Boris Rosing (Russian) applies for patent for system using mechanical scanner and cold CRT.
1910–1912	Vladimir Kosmo Zworykin is student of Rosing at Saint Petersburg Technological Institute.
1911	Rosing demonstrates TV system using rotating-mirror scanner and cold CRT.
1919	Zworykin immigrates to New York City.
1922	Charles Francis Jenkins (American) initiates work to develop radio broadcasting of movies to homes.
1922	March 13—Jenkins files for patent on mechanical TV system.
1923	Ernst Fredrik Werner Alexanderson (Swedish) working at General Electric Company discloses intent to develop radio transmission of moving pictures.
1923	December 29—Vladimir Kosmo Zworykin working at Westinghouse Research Laboratory applies for patent on all-electronic TV system.
1925	John Logie Baird (Scotsman) demonstrates television system in London.
1925	June—Jenkins demonstrates radio broadcasting of movies.
1925	Alexanderson demonstrates his system.
1927	April—Bell Labs demonstration of two-way television over wire between New York City and Washington, D.C.

1927	First TV license issued by FCC to Jenkins, station W3XK.
1927	Philo T. Farnsworth demonstrates his TV system, using image disector tube.
1929	January—Zworykin explains his ideas for TV to David Sarnoff of RCA. Later that year Zworykin comes to RCA to direct TV research.
1928	Bell Labs demonstrates color television (possibly 1929).
1929	November 16—Zworykin applies for patent on kinescope CRT.
1939	NBC begins TV broadcasting and RCA begins sale of TV sets.
1941	NTSC adopts 525-line and 30-frames/sec standard.
1941	NBC and CBS TV stations in NYC are first licensed by FCC.
1945	FCC allocates thirteen VHF stations (channel 1 later dropped).
1948	Ed Parsons of Astoria, Oregon, installs coaxial cable system to deliver distant TV received over the air from Seattle.
1950	Robert J. Tarlton of Lansford, Pennsylvania, installs cable TV system to deliver TV signals received from Philadelphia.
1950	FCC approves CBS field-sequential color TV.
1952	FCC allocates seventy UHF channels.
1953	FCC reverses decision and adopts NTSC color standard.
Late 1990s	High-definition digital television.

CHRONOLOGY

PHOTOGRAPHY CHRONOLOGY

1500s	Camera obscura devised.
early 1800s	Thomas Wedgwood experiments with silhouette images on silver-nitrate moistened paper.
1826	Joseph-Nicéphone Niépce makes first crude photograph with camera obscura.
1833	William Henry Fox Talbot discovers how to fix image on paper.
1839	Louis-Jacques-Mandé Daguerre reveals reversed-image, copper-plate, fixed process called daguerreotype.
1841	Patent issued to Talbot for process to produce paper positives from paper negative.
1846	Talbot used paper in camera obscura.
1861	James Clerk Maxwell invents three-additive-color process for projected images.
1878	Eadweard Muybridge made string-tripped photographs of galloping horse at Leland Stanford's farm.
1888	Thomas Alva Edison files caveat dated October 17 describing instrument to record motion—the "kinetoscope"—images on spiral on cylinder.
1888	George Eastman introduces $25 Kodak camera.
1889	George Eastman develops rolls of flexible celluloid film.
1891	Edison files patent on August 24 for 35 mm, film-based kinetoscope.
1893	Patents issued February 21 for camera, March 4 for viewer.
1893	C. Francis Jenkins projects moving images on a screen.
1894	*The Sneeze* film made by Edison.

1894	April 14—first peep-show parlor opened on Broadway in New York City—charged 5¢ per machine—the "Nickelodeon."
1894	Lumière brothers make first projector in Lyons, France.
1895	Jenkins demonstrates projected moving images at Exposition in Atlanta.
1895	February 13—Patent issued to Louis and Auguste Lumière for Cinématographe camera and projector —used triangular eccentric to move film.
1895	December 28—Lumières begin regular screenings.
1900	Brownie camera introduced for children.
1903	Edison's *The Great Train Robbery*—earns $2 million by 1908.
1905	Storefront movie theater opens in Pittsburgh—called "Nickelodeon."
1907	Lumière brothers develop three-color process using grains responsive to each color.
1908	First exterior movie shots made in Southern California.
1913	Edison adds sound to movies.
1915	Universal Studios opens at Lankershirm Boulevard in Southern California.
1928	Kodacolor film introduced.
1935	Kodachrome three-layer color film developed.
1947	Edwin Land's instant camera.
mid-1980s	Sony electronic camera.
late 1990s	Digital cameras.

CHRONOLOGY

FACSIMILE CHRONOLOGY

1842	Scotsman Alexander Bain uses electrical synchronization of two pendulums, one as a recorder and other as reproducer. British patent obtained in 1843.
1848	Cylinder/screw mechanism invented in England by Frederick Bakewell.
1885	Frenchman Clement Ader invents light valve for recording on photosensitive paper.
1888	Telautograph machine invented by Elisha Gray—predecessor to facsimile.
1902	German Arthur Korn demonstrates photoelectric scanning.
1910	Korn links Berlin with Paris by fax.
1922	Korn sends fax photo of pope from Rome to Maine by radio.
1924	RCA, AT&T, and Western Union all demonstrate fax systems, mostly for use by the press.
1934	Associated Press adopts AT&T system, calls it "Wirephoto."
1937	Fax radio newspapers start: WOR in New York City; KSTP in St. Paul; WGH in Norfolk, Virgina; WHO in Des Moines, Iowa.
1941	Over forty thousand fax receivers sold for use in homes.
1948	The *Chicago Tribune*, the *New York Times*, the *Miami Herald*, and the *Philadelphia Inquirer* are fax news broadcasting. *Inquirer* has an eight-page weekly edition; *Herald* has five editions daily.
1948	Eleven stations licensed for experimental fax broadcasts.
1950	Fax broadcasts all end!
1970s	New fax standards result in a fax rebirth and much growth.
1990s	Facsimile mostly displaced by e-mail.

II

COMPARING MEDIA

The second part of this book is concerned with the development of a taxonomy of communication media. The taxonomy attempts to define the various modalities, dimensions, and characteristics that can be used to categorize and compare communication media.

The taxonomy is developed in chapter 5. Chapter 6 then discusses the modality, purpose, and interactivity of communication media. The various dimensions involving the technological aspects of communication media are described in chapter 7. An appendix discusses the basic terms and concepts of modern electronic communication media and provides background for the non-engineer. The consumer perspective of communication media is covered in chapter 8. Various communication media are compared in chapter 9, and a theory to explain the use and evolution of media is developed in chapter 10.

The taxonomy developed in this part of the book is intended as a framework to discuss and explain media. The taxonomy is not intended to be a rigid classification scheme; the boundaries between various media can be very blurry at times.

A Taxonomy of Communication Media

COMMUNICATION AND MEDIA

The Shannon model of the communication process, mentioned in the introduction to this book, can be simplified to a source, a communication medium, and a receiver of the communication, as shown in figure 5.1. The message of the communication is conveyed over a medium, which can be either physical, natural, or electronic.

A person communicating face-to-face with another person is at the foundation of the communication process. This face-to-face communication depends primarily on the senses of vision, hearing, and touch. Communication also sometimes involves other sensory elements, such as smell, taste, and kinesthesia. Speech is communicated by sound and received by hearing, and text and writing are communicated on paper and received by sight. Moving and stationary images are also received by vision. Text, speech, and images will be referred to as communication modalities.

Sound and vision can be extended to conquer distance, to reach a large and widely scattered audience, and to conquer time. Communication media usually involve one or more of these extensions of natural media. The transmission of sound by radio signals is an example of the extension of a natural means of communication to conquer distance. Radio also allows one person to broadcast speech to a large and usually scattered audience. Mass production of newspapers and books also allows one person to reach a large audience. The storage of sound on compact discs conquers time.

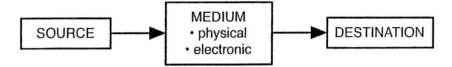

FIGURE 5.1
Simplified version of Shannon model of communication

Table 5.1 shows these extensions are either physically delivered or electronically delivered.

DIMENSIONS OF COMMUNICATION MEDIA

There are many ways in which communication media can be categorized, but not all are significant in developing an understanding of communication services. This chapter defines and describes a number of significant dimensions of communication media. Later chapters will use these dimensions to characterize current media and their uses and to project future uses and new media.

Directionality: Two-Way (Duplex) and One-Way (Simplex)

One significant dimension is the directionality of the communication. Strictly one-way communication is called *simplex communication*. Television and radio are strictly one-way media that are broadcast from one source to many destinations. A viewer may be aggravated over the content of a TV show, but there is no way to be heard at the studio, no matter how loudly the viewer shouts at the TV set.

Table 5.1. The extension of natural media and their modality of communication.

Natural Means of Communication	Modality	Extension	
		Physically Delivered	*Electronically Delivered*
sound	speech	audio recording	telephone
			radio
vision	text	books	telegram
		newspapers	e-mail
	image	photographs	facsimile
		movies	television
touch			"feelies"
smell		"scratch and sniff"	

Two-way communication is called *duplex communication*. Simultaneous two-way communication is called *full duplex communication*. Telephone service is a two-way medium that connects one phone with any other phone on this planet. Two-way communication in which only one-way communication is possible at a time is called *half duplex communication*.

Delivery: Physical and Electronic

TV and radio are delivered over the air as electronic signals. Other broadcast media, such as compact discs and videotapes, are delivered physically. Telephone service is an interactive, two-way, interpersonal form of communication that is delivered electronically. Mail service is a two-way, interpersonal form of communication that is delivered physically.

Audience: Broadcast and Narrowcast

Communication media that transmit information to many people are called *broadcast media*. Communication media that send information to a few people are called *narrowcast media*. Interpersonal communication media, such as the telephone, are used for one-to-one communication. The audience for the communication is usually just one other person, and there are two participants in the communication process. Teleconferencing enables a group of people to communicate; the audience is generally a few persons. Radio, television, and other mass media enable communication from one to many; the audience is many people.

Modality (Content)

The content or modality of the information can be categorized as image (moving and still), text, or audio (speech). Television involves moving images and audio. Radio and the telephone involve solely audio. Interpersonal mail, both physically delivered and electronic, is mostly text. Facsimile is an electronic, interpersonal medium for text and images.

Significant dimensions of communication media include

- directionality (one-way, two-way),
- purpose (entertainment, information),
- delivery mechanism (electronic, physical),
- audience (one-to-one, one-to-many), and
- modality or content (image, text, audio—either alone or in a mixture).

Media Map

The various communication media can be placed on a two-dimensional media map according to method of delivery (electronic or physical) and modality (text, speech or audio, moving images, and stationary images). The method of delivery is further subdivided by audience (one-to-one and one-to-many). Silent Radio was a method of sending a moving line of text to a number of locations; it will be described in more detail in a later chapter.

Purpose

Another significant dimension of communication media is the purpose for which they are intended. Communication can usually be categorized by purpose as either (1) entertainment or (2) information seeking and dissemination.

When a person watches a television movie or listens to a compact disc, it is reasonably clear that the prime purpose of the communication is entertainment. Television news shows might be watched to gain information, but the television stations are well aware of the importance of presenting news in an entertaining fashion. Are television news and newspaper reporting really just other forms of entertainment? You might argue that listening to the radio in the morning to check traffic conditions is information gathering. Calling a travel agent to make an airline reservation clearly is an example of using the telephone as an information tool. But talking by telephone for hours with a distant friend is an entertaining way to keep in contact and exchange information of what is happening. Obviously, forms of most communication can be used for more than one purpose.

The purpose of communication might be to persuade another person or many people to act or to think in a certain way. Propaganda is an example of communication intended to persuade and to control people. Interactive communication between the teacher and students in the classroom, the use of textbooks, and video teleconferencing for remote learning are examples of using communication to instruct and educate people. Clearly, there are many purposes for communication. Later we shall attempt to boil down the purposes to only two: to entertain or to inform.

Participation: Passive/Active

Some communication media involve the user in active participation, others do not. Television is mostly a passive medium for the viewer. The viewer passively stares at the screen or perhaps engages in another activity at the same time if the show is boring or during commercial breaks. The most interaction for most viewers is pushing the buttons on the remote control to change the channel.

Reading a book requires more active participation. Pages must be turned, and one must read the printed words and make some mental effort to grasp their meaning. Listening to music, too, can be an active experience. Teenagers dancing to pop and rock music are certainly involved physically in active participation.

The telephone requires active participation. One must listen attentively and respond appropriately. Reading a newspaper requires active involvement. What about listening to the radio? If the program is informative, the listener might be actively involved. If it is just background music, then no participation might occur at all. If it is lively dance music, a young person might participate by leaping from the couch to dance to the music.

Technology

There are a number of technological dimensions to communication media, some of which are touched on here and covered in more detail in a later chapter. Perhaps the most important technological dimension of communication is the bandwidth required to transmit or convey information.

Communication signals occupy a wide range of analog bandwidths and digital capacities. Communication services and media requiring large bandwidths are called *broadband media*, and those requiring small bandwidths are called *narrowband media*. But these terms are all relative, and care should be given to being specific in stating the actual bandwidths and capacities.

Conventional television is a broadband medium requiring a bandwidth of 4.5 MHz (4,500,000 hertz) for the video and audio signals. Telegraphy is a narrowband medium requiring only a few hundred hertz. Telephone service is a voice-band medium requiring 4,000 hertz in analog form and 64,000 bits per second in digital form. The stereo phonograph record contains two hi-fi signals, each with a maximum frequency of about 15 kHz (15,000 hertz). The compact disc contains two digital audio signals, each requiring 705,600 bits per second. The overall bit rate of the compact disc after including extra bits for error correction is 4,321,800 bits per second, requiring a bandwidth of about 2,000,000 hertz. The dial-up modems used with personal computers to access various database services over the Internet operate at bit rates as high as 56,000 bits per second. High-speed broadband access to the Internet (with cable or DSL modems) can be at rates of a few million bits per second.

Some Other Dimensions

Communication can be simultaneous, such as speaking on the telephone and watching television. Communication can also be delayed for hours, or even days, as with the telephone answering machine or the posting of a letter. This dimension of communication is called the *timing*.

Some communication media, such as books and magazines, use messages that exist in a tangible form. Such media are said to be *hard-copy media*. Other communication media generate messages that exist only for the moment, such as the sound of a radio show. Such communication media are called *soft-copy media*.

Communication can occur anywhere: at home, at work, or at some public place. Telephone booths are an example of a public place for telephone service. Movie theaters are public places for the viewing of motion pictures. The same movies can usually also be seen at home on the VCR or DVD machine or on CATV. The place where the communication occurs is another dimension of communication.

Communication involves messages and the exchange and transmission of information. The content of the information may be highly specialized, such as the fare for an airline trip. Or the content of the information can be of general interest, such as a weather forecast. The content of the communicated information is another dimension of communication.

Researchers have attempted to create taxonomies of communication. John A. Ciampa classifies communication into two broad categories: "immediate" and "mediate" (Ciampa 1988). His immediate category is comparable to what others call "face-to-face," and his mediate is comparable to what is usually called "mediated communication," namely the use of some medium of communication. Ciampa further divides immediate communication into "private" and "public," and mediate communication into "extension" and "storage." Extension involves the use of some form of electronic medium, such as radio waves or copper wire, and storage involves some form of what today is called "hard copy," such as paper or recording. Rudy Bretz classifies communication media broadly as "telemedia" and "recording media" (Bretz 1971). His telemedia is conventional telecommunication media "capable of transmitting programs across distance in real-time," and his recording media are physical media that capture programs. Bretz further classifies media according to the modality, such as sound or audio, picture, graphics, and print. Various kinds of motion are also encompassed in his taxonomy.

USE OF DIMENSIONS

Matrixes can be developed of groups of the various dimensions of communication and then filled in with specific services. This can be helpful in determining whether opportunities for new services exist. Such analysis will be performed in depth in later chapters, but a preview of what is entailed might be helpful.

For example, consider text as a broadcast medium delivered over the air. A few hundred pages of text are broadcast over the air along with the television signal during the time it takes for the beam to retrace itself vertically from the bottom to the top of the picture, the so-called *vertical blanking interval*. The textual information is general-interest information, such as news headlines, weather, and sports. The service, called *teletext*, is available in Europe, but not available or even known in the United States.

Another reason for studying dimensions of communication is to understand communication better. For example, the relationship between the purpose of communication and the bandwidth, or capacity, of the medium is quite interesting. It would seem that when the purpose of the communication is entertainment, we demand ever-increasing amounts of bandwidth. FM radio (200,000 Hz of radio-frequency spectrum) sounds better and is more enjoyable to listen to than AM radio (only 10,000 Hz of radio spectrum). The compact disc is much more entertaining than phonograph records. Color television is more enjoyable with prettier pictures than monochrome television. But program content and quality are certainly important as well. A modern digital recording of a poor performance of Mussorgsky's *Pictures at an Exhibition* is not as entertaining to me as an early 1950s analog, monophonic recording of Toscanini's great performance. So although bandwidth appears significant, there can be other dimensions that are more important.

However, when communicating to obtain information, bandwidth seems much less important. The telephone call replaces a face-to-face visit. Electronic mail replaces a telephone call. In general, entertainment means large bandwidths, while information seeking implies low bandwidths. And newer services appear to be confirming this model. High-definition television would require considerably more bandwidth than conventional television. Electronic mail requires less bandwidth than a telephone call.

The picturephone was an attempt at a high-bandwidth form of telecommunication for information seeking. It failed. Perhaps our examination of the relationship between bandwidth and the purpose of communication can help us understand why.

REFERENCES

Bretz, Rudy. *A Taxonomy of Communication Media*. Englewood Cliffs, N.J.: Educational Technology Publications, 1971.

Ciampa, John A. *Communication: The Living End*. New York: Philosophical Library, 1988.

Schramm, Wilbur. "Channels and Audiences." In *Handbook of Communication*, edited by Ithiel de Sola Pool et al. Chicago: Rand McNally, 1973, 160–174.

The Modality, Purpose, and Interactivity of Communication

THE MODALITY CIRCLE

Communication as discussed in this book is a human process. Most human communication is through sight and sound. Human speech encompasses communication that occurs primarily by sound between humans. Perhaps music should be included as another form of human communication that occurs through sound. Sight accounts for a considerable portion of human communication in the form of the written and printed word, graphics and stationary images (such as photographs and drawings), and moving images (such as movies and television).

There thus appear to be four major modalities of human communication:

- speech,
- text,
- stationary images, and
- moving images.

The four modalities of human communication can be arranged around a circle, as shown in figure 6.1, indicating the proximity of one to the other. In particular, text is a visual form of speech but is also a stationary image. Speech usually accompanies moving images, and both stationary and moving images are forms of communication by imagery. The circular arrangement appropriately indicates these proximities.

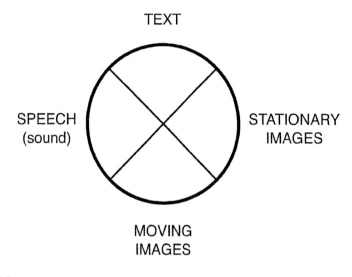

FIGURE 6.1
Modalities of human communication

BROADCAST ELECTRONIC MEDIA

Various broadcast electronic media can be placed within the modality circle, as shown in figure 6.2. The closeness of a medium to the line defining the quadrants of the circle indicates that the medium partially overlaps two modalities. Teletext is an example of a medium that consists mostly of text but also includes stationary images in the form of graphics.

INTERPERSONAL ELECTRONIC MEDIA

Various interpersonal electronic media can be placed within the modality circle, as shown in figure 6.3. Facsimile and the Internet use both text and stationary images, and hence are placed near the line between the two modalities.

PURPOSE

One of the most significant dimensions of communication media is the purpose of the communication it carries. There are many possible purposes for communication; some are obvious, such as to entertain and to be entertained, to obtain information and to disseminate information, and to teach and to learn. Communication media can be used to control a populace through propaganda or to garner votes through political broadcast.

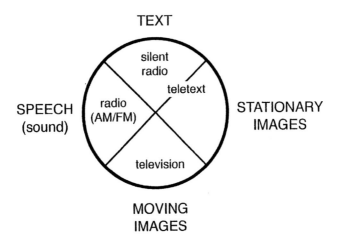

FIGURE 6.2
Broadcast electronic media

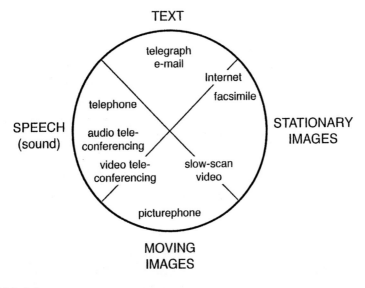

FIGURE 6.3
Interpersonal electronic media

Information

In the broadest sense, communication involves information. Thus, the dissemination and the reception of information have a lot to do with the purpose of communication, be it broadcast or interpersonal communication. We thus need to think about the purpose of communication from the perspective of information.

The term *information* is very broad and all-inclusive. Communication media are a way to obtain and to disseminate information of various kinds and for various purposes. All communication involves the transmission and reception of information. Most of us probably distinguish between seeking information for the purpose of adding to one's knowledge and turning to the media for entertainment. It is tempting therefore to try to fit the purpose of communication into one of two general categories: to inform or to entertain. Unfortunately, the world of communication is far too complex to be so simply categorized.

Entertain and Inform: A Blurred Categorization

Consider the simple activity of reading a newspaper. On one level, we read the newspaper to be informed. But on another level, we read the newspaper to be entertained. Advertisers want us to read their advertisements as a stimulus to buy their products. The success of *USA Today* comes partially from its ability to package information in such a way that is both entertaining and informative. Television is watched mostly for entertainment, but news programs inform us about world and local events. We probably watch the news to be informed, but we watch a movie or talk show to be entertained. However, television producers are well aware that even a news show must be both entertaining and informative to hold its audience.

There are many other reasons for watching television, and much research has been performed to determine these reasons. Clearly, the major reason for watching television or for going to the movies is our desire to be entertained. But we watch news shows to be informed. Serious drama and situation comedies help us understand human nature and social interactions. Nature shows tell us about the world in an entertaining way. Politicians appear on television programs to convince us to accept their positions on various issues or to impress us with their image. Thus, the purpose of a communication medium such as television can be quite extensive and blurred.

This blurring extends to interpersonal media as well. The telephone is a powerful medium for obtaining specific information, for instance, an airline departure time or the price of a shirt. However, we also chat on the telephone for hours with friends, and in this way, the telephone can be a source of entertainment.

Telephone chat lines are quite popular for dating and other purposes. Used this way, the telephone reaches a number of persons, which is quite different than its usual one-on-one function. In a sense, the telephone party line of the past has been resurrected. Similarly, CB radio can be listened to by many and also has a party-line aspect. The Internet is used for similar chat purposes, with text being the modality of the communication.

People seek information to become educated. Students attend classes at school or college and listen to and watch their instructors (I hope!). The educational process can be viewed as the communication of information from the instructor (or a textbook) to the student. Thus, the prime purpose of the educational process is to inform. However, motivation is a major part of learning and the resourceful instructor knows how to combine some entertainment with the flow of hard information. As a teacher, I know I am losing my students when I see one of them moving a finger as if attempting to use the remote control to change the TV channel—in this case, my lecture!

Conclusion

Undoubtedly, a vast array of purposes of communication could be listed. However, the two global categories "to entertain" and "to inform" seem most relevant. Yet, many communication media have purposes that extend across both global purposes, and some media have purposes that do not fit into either categorization.

INTERACTIVITY

Definition

Much attention today is given to so-called interactive media. But what exactly does *interactive* mean? In what sense are some media interactive while others are not? Are there different levels of interactivity?

The term *interactive* implies a communication situation in which an action that is performed causes another action to occur. In its broadest sense, almost everything we do is interactive since most actions cause another action to occur as a response. Pushing a button on the remote control causes the TV channel to change and thus can be considered to be an interactive process.

Some form of two-way communication is implied when an action by one participant is followed by a response from another. Clearly a conversation between two people is an interactive process, whether conducted face-to-face or over the telephone. But is writing a letter to one person and then receiving a reply somewhat later an interactive process? Does interactivity imply that the process must be instantaneous, or can the response be delayed in time?

Is reading a book an interactive process? A reader can turn pages at a leisurely pace and then jump ahead to read the end of the story, if impatient. The telephone clearly is an interactive communication medium since the use of the telephone involves speaking to another human being.

Does interactivity extend to our interactions with machines and with computers in particular? Do we interact with our personal computer while writing a letter? The computer user touches a key on the keyboard and obtains an instant response produced on the screen. But the user is in total control of the response, and there is no chance of any unexpected response, unless the user accidentally hits the wrong key. Since the response is known in advance, and no new or unexpected information flows to the user, this process is not interactive.

Is the use of the TV remote control an interactive process? The viewer presses a button and a response occurs. Yet, when tuning the dial of a TV set, the viewer knows what channel is being tuned to. Tuning is not an interactive process with the TV set. Since television is a one-way broadcast medium, it clearly is not an interactive medium.

But what about teletext? The information is sent along with the broadcast television signal. The transmission of the information in the teletext database clearly is a one-way process. But consider the complete process: the user enters a frame number into the handheld keypad, waits until the requested frame is received and decoded by the electronics in the TV set, and finally sees and reads the frame displayed on the screen. Information is contained in the frame, and interaction occurs between the entering of a frame number and the response in the form of a displayed frame on the TV screen. Although a broadcast service, teletext would thus seem to have an interactive aspect and should perhaps be considered an interactive medium. Dr. Martin C. J. Elton coined the term *pseudo-interactive* to characterize teletext.

An interactive communication process thus is a two-way exchange of information that can occur on an instantaneous or a delayed basis.

Interactivity/Modality

Speech over the telephone appears to be the most suitable modality for interactive interpersonal telecommunication. Text appears to be a suitable modality for noninteractive interpersonal telecommunication. Electronic mail, conventional mail, and facsimile are appropriate modalities for delayed interpersonal telecommunication. Telephone answering machines and voice mail are delayed forms of interpersonal telecommunication using the speech modality. Computer users can interconnect directly and exchange text messages in an interactive fashion—a service originally called *computer conferencing* and today known as *instant messaging*. The personal letter delivered by postal service is the medium of interpersonal communication by text, but the physically delivered letter is not a form of telecommunication. Table 6.1 shows various telecommunication media according to modality and interactivity.

Many people do not like talking to telephone answering machines. Computer conferencing was very awkward to me when I experimented with it many years ago. Often, I simply abandoned the computer communication and picked up the telephone. Today, instant messaging over the Internet is very popular with many people—but not with me.

Electronic mail used to be awkward to use and required considerable expertise in computers and data communication. The Internet and the World Wide Web changed all that, and e-mail is very simple to use and has achieved great popularity in recent years. Some people use the Internet to communicate in real time by text with others on the Net. But many people find such "chatting" by text to be very frustrating.

Table 6.1. Modality and interactivity of various communication media.

INTERACTIVITY	MODALITY	
	SPEECH	TEXT
INSTANTANEOUS	telephone	instant messaging
DELAYED	answering machine	e-mail
	voice mail	facsimile

Speech communication by telephone is the preferred modality of inter-active interpersonal telecommunication, and text communication by e-mail and facsimile are the preferred modality for delayed telecommunication.

Interactivity/Directionality

Most interactive communication media are transmitted over a two-way communication medium. The telephone is a two-way interactive communication medium. However, teletext is transmitted over the one-way broadcast medium of television, but is an interactive service.

7

Technology

BANDWIDTH

In terms of technology, bandwidth is probably the most significant factor. The directionality of the communication is another technological factor. Bandwidth is a measure of the signal-carrying capacity of a communication medium or channel but is also a measure of the spectrum space required by a signal.

Bandwidth is expressed in hertz, which is a measure of frequency, or how frequently a signal varies. A single telephone signal requires a bandwidth of 4,000 hertz (abbreviated 4 kHz, or 4 kilohertz), and a single conventional television signal requires a bandwidth of 4,500,000 hertz (abbreviated 4.5 MHz, or 4.5 megahertz).

Communication signals have waveforms, or waveshapes, that describe the variation of the signal over time. The direct characterization of this waveform is called an analog representation of the signal. Another way to represent the waveform is as a series of digits with each digit representing the amplitude of the waveform at particular instants in time. Such a representation is called digital. The digits are encoded as on/off, or 0/1, binary digits, or bits. The number of bits sent per second for a signal is a measure of the digital capacity of the signal. In the case of a communication medium or channel, the maximum number of bits per second is a measure of the digital capacity of the medium or channel.

Most communication signals are transmitted over some communication medium, such as radio waves or copper wire. Such signals frequently must be shifted in frequency to the appropriate space in the spectrum. Frequency shifting is accomplished by a technique called modulation. The original signal—in its most basic form before being shifted in frequency or otherwise changed—is called the *baseband signal*. Baseband signals can be either in analog form or in digital form.

Most signals have considerable redundancy. For example, if the vowels are left out of an English sentence, a reader can still usually decipher it. By removing the redundancy of a signal through appropriate processing, the signal can be compressed in terms of its bandwidth. Such compression is most easily performed with digital signals since digital computers can be used to perform the compression via appropriate rules, called *algorithms*. Most analog signals can also be compressed, but not as easily.

Table 7.1 gives the analog and digital bandwidths of a number of communication signals and services in both full and compressed forms.

DIRECTIONALITY

Some communication services are strictly one-way. They are broadcast usually from a single source to many recipients. Television is a one-way service. Other communication services are two-way. Most interpersonal communication services are two-way, such as telephone service.

Table 7.1.   Analog and digital bandwidths of major communication services and signals.

SERVICE	ANALOG		DIGITAL	
	full	compressed	full	compressed
telegraphy	<150 Hz		<300 bps	
telemetry	<150 Hz		<300 bps	
e-mail	4 kHz		1.2−9.6 kbps	
videotex	4 kHz		1.2−9.6 kbps	
voice telephony	4 kHz	200 Hz	64 kbps	1.2 kbps
facsimile	4 kHz		28.8 kbps	
slow-scan video	4 kHz		64 kbps	
AM radio station	10 kHz			
FM radio station	200 kHz			
videophone	1 MHz	4 kHz	4 Mbps	64 kbps
video	4.5 MHz		60 Mbps	128 kbps
teleconferencing				384 kbps
				1.5 Mbps
NTSC color TV	4.5 MHz		90 Mbps	3 Mbps
HDTV	20 Mhz		300 Mbps	45 Mbps

Table 7.2. Directionality of major communication services.

SERVICE	TWO-WAY	SWITCHED	ONE-WAY
telegraphy	X	X	
telemetry			X
e-mail/Internet	X	X	
videotex	X	X	
voice telephony	X	X	
facsimile		X	X
slow-scan video		X	X
AM radio			X
FM radio			X
videophone	X	X	
video teleconferencing	X		
NTSC color TV			X
HDTV			X
teletext			X

Some communication services can reach any one of many destinations; such services are said to be *switched*. The telephone is one clear example of a switched, two-way service. Table 7.2 gives the directionality of a number of communication services.

NETWORKS

Electronic communication signals are carried from one place to another over telecommunication networks. Broadcast networks are strictly one-way. CATV is an example of a one-way broadcast network. The CATV network has a tree structure. The main trunk flows from the treetop (called the head end), and branches flow down local streets and neighborhoods. The final twig (called the *drop*) goes to each home. Amplifiers are placed along the path every few thousand feet to increase the strength of the signal, and these amplifiers amplify in one direction only. However, CATV networks can be upgraded to create an upstream return capacity for two-way applications, such as cable modems.

The telephone network is an example of a switched two-way network. One telephone can reach any other telephone simply by dialing its number. A circuit—either real or virtual—is created between the two telephones, either by switching physical wires and channels carrying analog signals or by switching the time sequence of digital signals. The telephone network is a circuit-switched network. The actual path taken by the voice signals is different for each call depending upon the destination and the availability of facilities along the way. The telephone network is also two-way: a person can simultaneously speak and listen.

The characteristics of data traffic are quite different from those of voice traffic. Data consists of short bursts, frequently with lengthy sessions or holding time, although the total amount of data sent and received in bits might be relatively small. The short, bursty nature of data communication is best switched by packet switching. With packet switching, a relatively short burst of data bits is assembled into a packet and given its own unique header containing information to specify the source and destination. The packet is then examined by router switches and gradually switched over transmission paths until the final destination is reached.

The two basic types of networks are broadcast and switched. Broadcast networks are one-way; switched networks usually are two-way. Switched networks can be either circuit switched or packet switched. Whatever the configuration and type of network, signals are carried along it on various transmission media.

TRANSMISSION MEDIA

A variety of transmission media are available for sending telecommunication signals from one place to another. The oldest medium is metallic wire, usually copper, and in the mid-1800s telegraph signals were the first form of telecommunication to be carried over this wire. Later, telephone speech signals were also carried over the same wire. The copper wire was out in the open and was installed on wooden poles. Later, pairs of insulated copper wires were twisted together to form electrical transmission circuits that carried telephone signals from city to city and across the continent. Truly electronic telecommunication arrived with the invention of the triode vacuum tube by Lee De Forest in 1906. His invention allowed small signals to be amplified so that they could be carried and received over great distances. Many pairs of wires are combined together to form a cable, and many telephone and other signals are carried in a single cable.

A coaxial (also called a coaxial cable) has an inner conductor of copper wire surrounded by an outer conductor. This configuration of conductors creates a telecommunication circuit that has a much greater bandwidth than a simple twisted pair.

The bandwidth capacity of a twisted pair of copper wires is more than adequate for carrying a telephone signal from one's home over a few miles to the local central office of the telephone company. However, that pair does not have the capacity to carry many television signals over the same distance. Coaxial cable does. The coaxial cable used by the CATV company has enough capacity to carry as many as one hundred television signals, although amplification of these signals is required along the way.

Radio has been an important medium for carrying many different kinds of signals. Broadcast television and AM and FM signals are all carried by radio from the broadcasting station's antenna into our homes. Very high frequency radio, called *microwave radio*, was used by long-distance telephone companies to carry tens of thousands of telephone signals from antenna to antenna across the continent. Similar microwave radio signals are carried to and from communication satellites that orbit the earth above the equator.

The newest transmission medium is optical fiber, formed from flexible strands of pure glass as thin as one-tenth the diameter of a human hair. Optical fiber has a tremendous bandwidth, and its theoretical capacity extends to thousands of television signals or hundreds of millions of telephone signals! Although its tremendous capacities exceed our current needs, optical fiber clearly is the transmission medium of choice for the foreseeable future. It is free from noise and interference, requires much less amplification along the way than other media, and has great capacity. Optical fiber carries signals under oceans and across continents. Optical fiber is the backbone of many CATV systems, and it is also used by telephone companies to carry many telephone channels to the central office from local neighborhoods.

Computers in the home and office are interconnected through local area networks (LANs). Multiconductor copper wire is used for the popular Ethernet local area network. Infrared is used between laptop computers and personal digital assistants (PDAs). Wireless is increasingly being used between laptops and a receiver that connects to the Internet, either over DSL or a cable modem. Communication is from computer to computer, from computer to printers, and from computers to an Internet hub that connects to the Internet. Some people believe the power line in the home could be used for communication purposes within the home and possibly to connect the home to distant locations.

Electric power is carried from generating plants to homes and offices over copper wires and an electrical distribution system consisting of a series of voltage step-down transformers. The transformers prevent electric currents from combining to become so large as to require unpractical thickness of wire. But the electric power distribution system has been designed to carry electricity in one direction at a single frequency of 60 Hz in the United States. The use of the electric power line for two-way telecommunication would encounter challenging technical problems and thus is not practical.

Within the home, cordless phones use radio waves to transmit their signals. The TV remote control uses infrared to transmit its signals to the television set. The television set is connected, usually over copper cables, to the VCR machine and the DVD player.

STORAGE MEDIA

Communication signals and information can be stored on a wide variety of storage media. Perhaps the oldest storage media were the stone tablets and early cave paintings used by prehistoric people. Printed matter is stored on paper in books, newspapers, and magazines. Photographs are a form of storing visual images. Sounds, such as music and memorable speeches, are recorded and stored on magnetic tape either in the form of exact replicas of the original waveforms (analog recording) or in the form of digits that represent the original waveforms (digital recording). All of these forms of storing text, images, and sounds are referred to as *hard copy* since the storage media are long lasting and tangible.

The advent of the digital computer created a new form of storing signals and information. This form is called *soft copy*, since the information is stored in a form that does not last. Computers encode and store information in the form of bits: a simple on/off, or 1/0, encoding of information. Such information can be stored temporarily in the memory of the computer or written onto computer disks and tape for more permanent storage. Most information stored in computers is text. A single alphanumeric character is encoded using 8 bits, and such an 8-bit cluster of information is called a *byte*. Floppy disks of the 3½-inch and the 5¼-inch varieties are magnetic storage media, and can be written and read by a computer. These disks typically store a few hundred thousand bytes of information. Without conversion by a computer, they are unintelligible to humans.

The 4¾-inch compact disc (CD) used to store audio signals can also be used to store text and graphic information. Used that way, the disc is called a *CD-ROM*. ROM stands for *read-only memory*, since the CD can be read only by the user's computer. The CD-ROM is a means of delivering vast quantities of information to the user: typical CD-ROMs can store about 700 million bytes—the equivalent of all the text in two thousand three-hundred-page books. The CD-ROM creates the possibility for electronic books and electronic encyclopedias.

Soft-copy media are usually displayed on computer screens. Although acceptable in work situations, such screens are not as user-friendly as paper-based media. It is difficult to envision curling up in front of the fireplace with a CRT version of a favorite novel.

TRENDS
The speed at which technology is progressing makes it difficult to predict its future developments and trends. However, one trend in transmission technology is quite clear: available bandwidth will continue to increase in capacity while simultaneously decreasing in cost. Optical fiber is the main impetus for this trend in transmission technology. Transmission is a major technological component of both broadcast and switched communication media, such as CATV, telephony, and the Internet.

Switched communication media, such as telephony, involve the use of switching machines. In the past, these switching machines used electromechanical technology that was inflexible. Today's switching machines are electronic and are controlled by programmable computers. The sophistication and flexibility of these computers make possible a host of new highly functional services. This trend will continue, and the challenge will be to use increased functionality in ways that create meaningful and useful new services for consumers.

TECHNOLOGY ENHANCEMENTS
The two major trends in communication technology have been increased bandwidth and increased functionality. These trends have interesting consequences for entertainment media and for interpersonal informative media. Table 7.3 suggests the impact of these trends.

Picturephone service requires considerable bandwidth, but its market failure implies that increased bandwidth is not relevant to interpersonal

Table 7.3. Impact of major trends in communication technology.

	ENTERTAINMENT (broadcast)	INFORMATIVE (interpersonal)
INCREASED BANDWIDTH (optical fiber)	HDTV	videophone *No!*
INCREASED FUNCTIONALITY (computer control)	videotex *No!*	call-waiting paging call-screening messaging e-mail World Wide Web

communication services that are primarily intended to inform. Videotex was marketed as an entertaining way to obtain access to all the world's information on the home TV set, but its market failure implies that increased functionality is not relevant to entertainment media. The Internet and the personal computer to access the World Wide Web are effective ways to obtain information, but their use as entertainment media is questionable. Yet there continue to be attempts to force interactive TV on consumers, who thus far do not seem interested.

BANDWIDTH COMPRESSION

In many cases, the bandwidth of the basic baseband signal can be reduced, or compressed, through appropriate signal processing. The signal processing removes redundancy in the baseband signal. The compressed signal is then transmitted to the destination where the redundant information is reconstructed to create the original baseband signal. Bandwidth compression has been suggested for use with telephone signals, but the cost of the processing has not decreased to keep pace with the increase in available transmission bandwidth. Compression of the speech signal is used for digital cellular wireless services, where radio spectrum is very limited. Video is another area where bandwidth compression is particularly useful.

Full-motion video is very costly in terms of bandwidth, requiring 4.5 MHz each direction or a bit rate of about 90 Mbps in digital form. Very costly transmission facilities are needed to carry such large amounts of bandwidth. Since there is little change from video frame to video frame and also because repetitive patterns occur within a frame, the transmitted image can be compressed in bandwidth, although smearing might occur if too much of the image changes too quickly. This trade-off is usually quite acceptable for most video imagery. Today, compression technology is used to reduce the video bit rate to a few Mbps, or even less, for DVDs.

There is redundancy in other communication signals as well. Text has redundancy. The 8 bits used per alphanumeric symbol in ASCII could easily be reduced to about 4 bits per symbol for most texts with suitable processing. In most cases, the additional processing to reduce redundancy to save bandwidth for the transmission and the storage of many signals is too costly. Video is one major exception.

Telephone speech is compressed to about 10,000 bits per second for digital cellular wireless service. However, compression is a compromise with quality, and thus in some circumstances the quality of the transmission suffers. Also, delay is required in the compression process, which can be troublesome in maintaining two-way communication. Music audio signals can be compressed, as they are in MP3, to as little as 32,000 bits per second, while maintaining very good quality.

8

Consumer Perspectives

The consumer is a key factor in determining the success—or the failure—of communication products and services in the marketplace. A number of communication products and services are examined in this chapter to determine the specific features that seem to have led to consumer acceptance and market success.[1] After examining these areas, some overall conclusions are made regarding the consumer driving forces that lead to success. These consumer driving forces might be useful for making predictions about the success of future communication products and services.

Clearly, the price of a particular product strongly affects the decision by a consumer to make or not to make a purchase. Transistors and large-scale integrated circuits have had considerable impact on reducing the cost of communication products and services. However, the analyses presented in this chapter do not treat prices in any detail.

TELEVISION

Television in many ways is really little more than old-fashioned radio, with moving pictures added. When seeking entertainment, consumers seem to demand as much sensory appeal as possible, and since the eye is the dominant sensory organ, television has enjoyed great success. Black-and-white television was supplanted by color television, probably because of its increased sensory appeal.

Like many areas of consumer electronics, television has two aspects: hardware (the TV set), and software (TV programming). Consumers seem to want quality in program content, but this does not necessarily equate with culture and art. They also appear to want considerable variety in programming; hence the addition of the UHF spectrum and the success of CATV, VCRs, and DVDs.

Consumers also seem to respond positively to the technical quality of TV receivers. The transistorization of TV receivers eliminated the frequent replacement of vacuum tubes and also improved the quality of the picture. Single gun and in-line gun picture tubes along with superior phosphors also offered improvements in the quality of the displayed image. Newer TV sets include electronic circuitry to correct color distortions during transmission of the NTSC signal used in the United States. These color-tracking circuits improve the image quality of the picture.

Small, portable television sets using flat LCD displays are quite popular. These small sets allow portable, personal viewing. Large-screen TV sets with stereophonic sound are available, but consumer demand thus far is limited. Large-screen TV sets also seem to offer increased sensory appeal. With small TV sets, TV viewing has become personal, and the family gathering around to watch the TV set might well be long past. However, large-screen TV displays might herald a return to family and group viewing.

The consumer driving forces for television appear to be increased sensory appeal, improved image quality, personal use, on-demand use, ease of use, and increased variety of program sources.

CATV

The term *CATV* originally stood for *community antenna television* and was initially introduced in rural areas. A high antenna picked up distant TV signals that were then distributed over a coaxial cable to homes in the community that otherwise would not be able to receive television. Later, the term *CATV* came to mean cable television used in urban areas to eliminate ghosts caused by multiple reflections of the broadcast TV signal and to improve image quality.

Unlike over-the-air television, which is free, CATV charges a monthly fee. CATV originally promised commercial-free TV, but commercials are appearing more frequently on CATV. R- and X-rated movies on CATV offered programming that was not available from broadcast network television. Today's CATV systems offer as many as two hundred channels to choose from. However, VCRs, rented tapes, and DVDs also expand variety for the consumer.

The consumer driving forces for CATV are improved reception, program variety, and specialized programming.

VIDEO RECORDERS AND PLAYERS

Videocassette recorders gave rise to home video libraries and the rental, exchange, and copying of videocassettes of movies and other programs. VCRs are used to record popular TV shows for later viewing at more convenient times. Videocassettes offer the consumer a variety of program material that can be viewed at any time and as often as desired. Digital storage devices (such as the TiVo recording box) enable favorite shows to be recorded and viewed later.

The videodisc was introduced to the consumer in the early 1980s but was withdrawn a few years later after suffering poor consumer acceptance. Videodisc players were not able to record TV shows and thus could not offer the time displacement possible with VCRs. Videodiscs were introduced again in the early 1990s, offering better picture quality than most cassettes. But the tremendous market penetration of VCRs was formidable. Furthermore, the discs were large and bulky at a time when small compact discs and smaller cassettes appeared to be the norm.

The digital video disc (DVD) was introduced at the very end of the 1990s. The DVD is the same small size as the audio CD and offers quality and convenience far superior to prerecorded VCR cassettes. Within a few years, the DVD has become so successful that the prerecorded VCR tape is facing the same fate as the phonograph record. Newer DVD players are also able to record DVDs, thereby stimulating illegal copying.

The consumer driving forces for VCRs and DVDs are increased variety of program material, time displacement of conventional broadcast TV, and on-demand viewing.

RADIO

FM radio offered a great improvement in sound quality over AM radio. Not only was noise and static reduced, but the frequency response of the audio signal was greatly extended and stereophonic audio was available. Clearly FM radio offered an increase in sensory appeal. The attempt to improve the quality of AM through the addition of stereo was not successful, mostly because of the poor frequency response of the audio signal and the noise and static encountered with AM radio.

Transistors have resulted in an improvement in quality and a decrease in both cost and size. Easier tuning is made possible by improved electronic circuitry and displays. Lightweight headsets allow personal listening.

The consumer driving forces for radio are improved quality, increased sensory appeal, portability, and personal listening.

AUDIO

Edison's cylinder was replaced by Berliner's disc—one of the first in a long series of improvements in the quality of the reproduction of recorded sound. The 78 rpm disc was then replaced by the 33⅓ rpm long-playing record, which later became extended to include two-channel stereophonic sound. And today the long-playing black vinyl record has been replaced by the compact disc with its digital representation of the sound signal. The improvements in frequency response, signal-to-noise ratio, dynamic range, and longevity of the recording medium are all apparent to consumers and result in much greater sensory appeal.

Not only has the software been improving in quality, but the audio equipment used to reproduce the sound has also been steadily improving in quality. Loudspeakers have become smaller in size but better in the quality of the sound. Headphones are lightweight yet offer outstanding sound quality.

Four-channel quadraphonic audio was introduced in the early 1970s and was soon withdrawn because of a lack of consumer acceptance. One reason was that any improvement in sound quality was barely noticeable, and also the use and placement of four loudspeakers was too complicated and costly.

The large, bulky reel-to-reel tape recorders of the past were replaced by small, portable audiocassette recorders. Sony's Walkman tape units offered portability and personal listening. Digital audiotape offers even smaller cassettes with much higher quality. The bandwidth of digital audio can be compressed using MP3 and other algorithms and then played on small players (such as the Apple iPod player) offering quality sound and small size.

The consumer driving forces in audio are program variety, quality, personal listening, on-demand listening, and portability.

Many consumers spend much time commuting to and from work in their automobiles, and hence auto audio is a source of much entertainment. The consumer driving forces for auto audio are not different from regular audio and are a variety of program sources, on-demand use, and improved quality.

Increased sensory appeal is also important, although the noisy environment of the car limits the impact.

PHOTOGRAPHY

Black-and-white photographs evolved to color, thereby offering an increase in sensory appeal and realism. Polaroid brought instant gratification to photography. The camcorder, with its instant viewing, supplanted 8 mm home movies. Sophisticated electronics in cameras make cameras easy to use, as exemplified by today's small, self-focusing, auto-loading 35 mm cameras.

New digital still cameras that record images on magnetic disks were introduced. The disks could be viewed on the home TV set or printed using a special adapter. These magnetic disk cameras offered instant viewing, but a TV set was needed and quality was lacking. Today's digital camera connects to the personal computer offering the consumer considerable quality, the ability to crop and modify the image, and the ease of printing to a high-quality color ink-jet printer. The pictures can also be sent over the Internet to family and friends.

The driving forces for photography are improved quality, ease of use, portability, and instant viewing.

TELEPHONY

Repertory dialers make it easy to reach frequently dialed numbers. Answer-and-record machines allow the consumer to listen on demand to calls that otherwise would be missed. Cordless telephones offer the benefit of portability. With improved microphones and with digital transmission, sound quality has become better than in the past.

Citizens band (CB) radio was primarily used in automobiles. Cellular wireless telephone service is far better since cellular connects to the telephone network. CB offered security while driving and was a source of personal information about traffic conditions, street instructions, and police-radar locations. Cellular wireless satisfies nearly all these needs in a pocket-sized cell phone that can be used anywhere. But when used in an automobile, some states now mandate the use of hands-free headsets. Digital wireless compresses the speech signal, thereby reducing the technical quality and causing delay. But technical quality is not as important to telecommunication consumers as convenience and accessibility.

The consumer driving forces for wireless and cellular radio are security and on-demand, personal, timely information.

VIDEOTEX, TELETEXT, AND THE INTERNET

Videotex was an interactive information service that gave access over telephone lines to a large, centrally located, computerized database containing a wealth of information and other services. The information was displayed on the home TV set. Videotex did not meet with much consumer acceptance—either in its original market introduction about twenty-five years ago or in its more recent version, called *WebTV*. One problem was the use of the home TV set for display, since this interferes with viewing TV shows. The home TV set is used mostly to view TV programs and also does not have much resolution, particularly when compared to a computer display.

Teletext transmits a few hundred frames of information over the air along with the regular TV signal. Teletext offers instant access to timely information of mass market appeal such as news, weather, traffic conditions, sports scores, and TV listings. Teletext has been successful in many countries, but is not available in the United States.

The Internet and the World Wide Web offer access to all sorts of information. All that is required is a personal computer and access to a telecommunication network. This access could be a simple dial-up modem that connects to the telephone line or some higher-speed connection through either a cable modem connecting to the CATV network or a digital subscriber line (DSL) connecting to the telephone network.

The consumer driving force for videotex, teletext, and the Internet is instant access to timely information. The success of teletext and the failure of videotex indicates that the large, centralized database of videotex was too difficult to access and search for many consumers. The Internet or World Wide Web solved this problem through the use of hypertext and search engines—thus its great success.

AUDIOTEX

Audiotex is the use of a touchtone telephone to interact with computerized databases. The requested information is returned to the user in the form of synthesized speech. Audiotex is easy to use and requires no special skills or training. It is also ubiquitous and requires no special hardware.

Cell phones offer access to people by voice communication. Adapting audiotex to convert Internet information to speech and also to recognize human speech to specify what information is desired makes access to the Internet possible over the cell phone. A user can make a cell phone call to determine the nearest restaurant specializing in a certain cuisine and price range. Directions to the restaurant would then be spoken back over the cell phone.

COMPUTERS

The home computer is often used as a word processor and thus simply is an improved replacement for the home typewriter. The home computer can also be used to send and receive e-mail and to search databases by accessing the World Wide Web over the Internet. Increasingly, digital cameras and MP3 audio players are being connected to the home computer, making it the center for the management of much home entertainment—a digital media management center. The home computer is an example of a single product that has many different uses.

The handheld personal digital assistant (PDA) offers access to computer power while on the move. Date books, addresses, and other information are always available, in the pocket. Wireless PDAs connect to the Internet so that stock prices, e-mail, and other timely information can be accessed anywhere at any time. The cell phone and the PDA might well converge into a single unit offering voice and text wireless access to people and information—all the time, anywhere.

CONCLUSION

The consumer benefits and driving forces that appear to be common to most entertainment-oriented communication products and services are

- increased sensory appeal,
- improved quality,
- ease of use,
- portability,
- personal use,
- increased program variety, and
- on-demand use.

When being entertained, the consumer appears to demand as much sensory input as possible, perhaps because an experience close to reality is desired. This does not seem to be the case when information seeking. The telephone, the telegraph, and facsimile do not deliver much sensory input. The information content of most messages is quite small and can be easily conveyed over narrowband telecommunication media. That clearly is not the case for entertainment media. FM radio, color television, and digital audio are all broadband communication media.

TOO MUCH VARIETY

Variety of choice appears to be a major consumer driving force in many communication products and services. An interesting question is whether too much variety can be self-defeating and can become a negative factor in influencing consumer purchases. Too much variety might confuse the consumer with too many alternatives thereby making a decision too difficult.

A possible example of too much variety was videotex, in which the sheer size and complexity of the database might have been too much for the consumer to comprehend and to find the desired information. With videotex, all the information was stored in one central database. Today, the World Wide Web has decentralized information and stores it throughout the world in many small databases, each separately maintained. Most importantly, the search engines of the Internet make it fairly easy to find information.

NOTE

1. Much of the material in this chapter is based on a study I performed while I worked at AT&T and which I reported in a memorandum entitled "A View of Consumer Electronics," dated August 16, 1982.

9

Media Comparisons

Earlier chapters developed and described the dimensions that can be used to characterize communication media. This chapter compares various communication media in terms of the more significant of these dimensions. Some specific comparisons that are made are audience and delivery, modality and delivery, and modality and purpose. Various forms of visual communication are also discussed and compared in this chapter.

AUDIENCE/DELIVERY
The intended audience for a communication can be

- one other person,
- a group of only a few other persons, or
- a large audience of many persons.

A large audience of many persons is usually called a *mass audience*, and mass media are used to communicate with such mass audiences. Communication can be delivered to these various audiences either physically or by telecommunication.

Table 9.1 shows the relationship between the method of delivery and the audience for various communication media. All possible audiences are served by both physical and telecommunication delivery of the communication.

Table 9.1. Relation between the size of the audience and method of delivery for various media.

AUDIENCE	DELIVERY	
	physical	telecommunication
one person	mail	telephone
		e-mail
few persons	bulletin board	telephone chat line
		CB radio
		conference call
		Internet chat room
many persons	junk mail	AM/FM radio
		television

VISUAL COMMUNICATION

This section examines visual communication and various methods of delivery. The content of visual communication includes

- moving images,
- still images, and
- text.

This content can be delivered electronically or physically over a variety of one-way broadcast media and two-way interpersonal media.

Motion pictures are delivered physically; television images are delivered electronically. Broadcast television can be delivered over the air, as in VHF and UHF television, or transmitted over coaxial cable, as in CATV. The picturephone uses moving images for interpersonal telecommunication. Moving images are recorded on film, as in motion pictures, on videotape, as in the videocassette recorder (VCR), or digitally, on a variety of physical media.

Still images can be captured on photographic film or on paper and can be delivered by hand or by post. Electronic delivery of still images is accomplished by facsimile transmission over the switched telephone network. Facsimile is mostly an interpersonal form of communication, although a broadcast form of facsimile for the delivery of a fax newspaper was tried in the early 1940s. It failed when television was introduced.

Text can also be sent by facsimile transmission. However, text is usually entered into a computer on a keyboard and is stored in the form of 8-bit ASCII characters. The digitized text can then be sent over the telephone network, or a data network, as e-mail. Text can also be sent along with a broadcast TV signal—a service known as teletext. The use of text as a form of communication is described in more detail in a following chapter on computer communication.

The various media for electronic delivery and physical delivery of visual communication are analyzed and summarized below.

Television is the broadcast form of communication of moving images over electronic delivery. Text is broadcast along with the TV signal by teletext. The picturephone is the one-on-one, or interpersonal, form of communication of moving images. Facsimile is a form of electronic delivery of still images and text. The fax newspaper was a broadcast form of facsimile that was tried in the early 1940s and abandoned with the advent of television. The interpersonal communication of text is through facsimile and e-mail. Video teleconferencing using moving images enables communication among a few participants. Computer bulletin boards are used to post electronic messages for an intended few recipients, and newer forms are known as blogs. Facsimile is sometimes used to send still images to a few recipients using a programmed dialer to call all the parties one by one. The Internet is also used by some people to distribute photographs to family members and friends.

The various visual communication media are classified according to content and their nature (broadcast/interpersonal) in table 9.2.

Movies are the broadcast form of moving images using physical delivery. Still images are broadcast in magazines through physical delivery. Photographs are a form of interpersonal communication. Text is physically delivered to many people through newspapers and junk mail, and increasingly

Table 9.2. Electronically delivered media classified by content and nature.

CONTENT	ELECTRONIC DELIVERY		
	Broadcast (one-to-many)	Interpersonal	
		one-to-one	one-to-few
Moving Images	television	videophone	video teleconferencing
Still Images	fax newspaper	facsimile	(facsimile) (Internet)
Text	teletext	e-mail facsimile	bulletin board blog

Table 9.3. Physically delivered media classified by content and nature.

CONTENT	PHYSICAL DELIVERY	
	Broadcast (one-to-many)	Interpersonal (one-to-one)
Moving Images	movies	
Still Images	magazines	photographs
Text	junk mail	letters
	newspapers	

through junk e-mail. The physically delivered letter is the most private form of interpersonal communication of text. The various physically delivered media are classified by content and nature in table 9.3.

MODALITY/DELIVERY

Communication media can be delivered from the source to the recipient either by physical delivery or through telecommunication over an electronic channel. Recorded media, such as compact discs, videocassettes, and digital video discs are delivered physically, in most cases, by the consumer who visits the store and purchases or rents the product. Books, magazines, and newspapers are also delivered physically to the consumer by post or by delivery services.

Radio and television are broadcast entertainment media that are delivered by telecommunication in the form of electronic signals, which are transmitted over the air by radio waves. Telegraphy, telephony, e-mail, and facsimile are interpersonal media that are delivered by telecommunication channels. Recorded audio, particularly pop songs, are being increasingly delivered by telecommunication over the Internet.

Table 9.4 shows the relationship between the method of delivery and the modality of various communication media.

MODALITY/PURPOSE

The two main purposes of communication are to entertain and to inform. Three main modalities of communication are audio, visual, and touch. Table 9.5 shows the relationship between the modality and the purpose of communication. Various communication media are indicated.

One interesting conclusion from this representation is that the visual modality is used mostly in the form of moving images for entertainment

Table 9.4.   Relation between delivery method and modality of various communication media.

MODALITY	DELIVERY	
	Physical	*Telecommunication*

Visual	• recorded
	  - VCR tape
	  - DVD
	• movies
	• print
	  - books
	  - newspapers
	• mail/letters
		• telegraph
		• e-mail
		• facsimile
		• videophone
		• teletext
		• television

Audio	• recorded
	  - LP/CD
	  - cassettes
		• radio
		  - AM
		  - FM
		• telephone
		• audiotex
		• Internet

Table 9.5.   Relationship between modality and purpose of communication.

MODALITY	PURPOSE	
	Entertain	*Inform*

Audio	• radio
	  - AM
	  - FM
	• recorded
	  - LP record
	  - CD
	  - cassette
		• telephone
		• audiotex

Visual	• television
	• recorded
	  - VCR tape
	  - DVD
	• movies
		• telegraph
		• e-mail
		• print
		  - books
		  - magazines
		• facsimile
		• Internet/Web
		• teletext

	VIDEO (moving images)	TEXT PHOTOS GRAPHICS
Touch	"feelies"	

purposes. The visual modality is used mostly as text, photos, and graphics for the exchange of information.

The touch modality has been added, mostly for academic purposes. The "feelies" were suggested by Aldous Huxley in the 1930s as a futuristic new form of entertainment medium, although they were never implemented (Huxley 1932). In 1970, I investigated a form of "feelies" using a tactile device, along with computer graphics, for interaction with a computer and also for interpersonal communication (Noll 1972). More recently, head-mounted displays sometimes coupled with tactile devices have been constructed to give the user a feeling of "virtual reality."

REFERENCES

Huxley, Aldous. *Brave New World*. New York: Doubleday, 1932.

Noll, A. Michael. "Man-Machine Tactile Communication." *SID Journal* 1, no. 2 (July/August 1972): 5–11.

Bandwidth

This chapter discusses the relationship between bandwidth and the purpose of communication for a variety of communication media. A theory explaining the success or failure of some communication media is developed from an analysis of the relationship between bandwidth and purpose.

BANDWIDTH/PURPOSE

Electronic communication media require bandwidth, either in the form of analog frequency space (hertz) or of digital capacity (bits per second). The bandwidth in hertz for various communication media and services are arrayed in figure 10.1. The scale starts at the top with such broadband services as CATV and over-the-air television and ends at the bottom with such narrowband services as telegraphy and telemetry.

At the broadest, most basic level, communication serves either to entertain or to inform. Entertainment media—such as radio, television, compact discs, movies—are usually broadcast on a one-way basis from one source to many recipients. Informative media for interpersonal communication are usually two-way interactive, on a one-to-one basis. Figure 10.1 is intriguing in that all the broadband services and media are one-way broadcast entertainment media and nearly all the narrowband services are two-way interpersonal informative media. This suggests a relationship between bandwidth and the purpose of communication.

The relationship between the purpose of communication and bandwidth for various electronic media is shown in figure 10.2.

CATV coaxial cable		1,000,000,000 Hz	**Broad**
VHF/UHF TV station	B	6,000,000 Hz	**Band**
digital audio (CD)	A	2,000,000 Hz	
FM radio station	N	200,000 Hz	
audio recording	D	20,000 Hz	
AM radio station	W	10,000 Hz	
telephone circuit	I	4,000 Hz	
facsimile	D	4,000 Hz	
e-mail	T	2,000 Hz	
telegraphy	H	1,000 Hz	**Narrow**
telemetry		400 Hz	**Band**

FIGURE 10.1
Bandwidth in hertz for communication media and services

BANDWIDTH

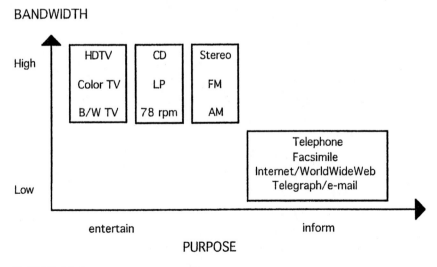

FIGURE 10.2
Relationship between purpose and bandwidth for various electronic media

The bandwidth of informative interpersonal media, such as the telephone and facsimile, has remained fairly constant over time. However, the bandwidth of entertainment media has increased steadily. More interestingly, entertainment media in general require much more bandwidth than informative media. It would appear that when being entertained, people demand as much high-quality acoustic and visual stimulation as possible, and that stimulation requires bandwidth. However, when communicating to exchange or obtain information, people need very little bandwidth. They want "just the facts," but they also want them quickly. Thus bandwidth is needed so that pages of information accessed over the Internet and World Wide Web arrive as fast as possible.

This model offers a possible explanation for the failure of the picturephone. The picturephone was intended as an extension of the telephone—an informative medium of communication. However, the picturephone used a large amount of bandwidth, more like an entertainment medium. This attempt to move an informative medium into the bandwidth space occupied by entertainment media was clearly an error.

Today, the Internet is being proposed as a medium to deliver broadband video to the home, possibly in some interactive fashion. Since the Internet basically is used to obtain access to information, this attempt to force it into carrying broadband entertainment might fail. Consumers become confused when a service intended mostly for information access is also promoted for entertainment purposes. The all-in-one information/entertainment appliance might simply be far too confusing for most consumers.

DIGITAL COMPRESSION

Compression technology has an impact on the above generalities about bandwidth. About twenty hours of music can be stored on a CD using MP3 and other forms of digital compression. Users can decide what music to compress and store on their personal music CDs.

The quality of compressed music using MP3 is virtually indistinguishable from the original, and any small compromise in quality is overcome by the benefits of nearly twenty times as much music on a CD. Furthermore, since the user decides what music to compress and store, the CD is very personal. All this is in consonance with the consumer driving forces for stored music: high quality, small size, and personal nature. MP3 music will surely be successful, whether stored on a CD or on some new medium in the future.

TRENDS

It seems that sensory appeal is related to the bandwidth of the signal. The more bandwidth, the more higher frequencies in recorded audio, the more color and resolution in television, and the more capacity for additional channels (like stereo).

First, consider television. There has been a steady growth in sensory appeal and bandwidth over time for television. Newer forms of television, such as high-definition television (HDTV) and 3-D TV, would offer even more sensory appeal. These improvements would require more bandwidth for the basic signal, although some form of compression might be used to transmit the signal.

A similar increase over time in sensory appeal and bandwidth occurs with recorded-audio media. A small solid-state chip (such as used in the Apple iPod Shuffle music player) can store all the digital information of a compact disc and in the future will probably store even more recorded material.

The conclusion is that entertainment media have experienced growth in bandwidth and sensory appeal over time. Consumers respond positively to increased sensory appeal in entertainment media.

Growth in bandwidth and sensory appeal does not seem to have occurred with interpersonal communication media. The telegraph has not changed bandwidth since its invention. The basic 4 kHz bandwidth of a telephone channel has been unchanged for many decades. E-mail is a newer form of interpersonal communication, but the bandwidth required is even less than that of the telephone. Digital cellular telephone service compresses the speech signal to a much lower bit rate than for conventional telephone service and also with lower quality. If there is any trend in interpersonal communication media, it is toward decreased bandwidth. The conclusion is that bandwidth and sensory appeal are not important for interpersonal communication media.

The telephone is a very functional means of communication, and functionality is an important component of telephone service. In the early days of telephone service, human beings operated the equipment that connected one party to another. These human operators responded to the callers, took messages, and forwarded calls. The human touch was lost when the switching function was automated with electromechanical switching technology. The automation, however, made telephone service more affordable, and hence more universal. Today, switching systems are electronic and are controlled by programmable digital computers that provide increased functionality.

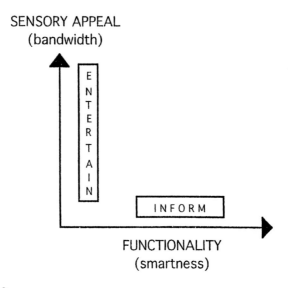

FIGURE 10.3
Relationship between sensory appeal and functionality for different communication purposes

Television and other broadcast media offer little or no functionality. Viewers and listeners passively watch or listen to broadcast media. Most entertainment media are low in functionality and high in bandwidth. In contrast, most interpersonal informative media are high in functionality and low in bandwidth. This relationship is shown in figure 10.3.

This relationship possibly helps explain the market failure of the picturephone and of videotex. As mentioned above, the picturephone was intended for interpersonal communication: a low-bandwidth, high-functionality form of communication. The attempt to make this communication high in bandwidth by the addition of the visual image simply was not consistent with the bandwidth requirements of interpersonal communication. Videotex was initially positioned as an adjunct to television through the use of the home TV set as the display device. Thus, television was being forced to have high functionality, in violation of the relationship.

The Internet and the World Wide Web are becoming increasingly more prevalent forms of communication, both for e-mail and for accessing information. They are discussed in more detail in a later chapter on computer communication.

III

ANALYZING MEDIA

Part III of this book applies the previously developed taxonomy to the analysis of communication media. Chapter 11 employs the taxonomy to compare the significant dimensions of a number of new communication services. The Internet and the World Wide Web are forms of communication involving the use of computers, and they are described and compared in chapter 12, although some elements were touched upon in earlier chapters.

Communication media are sometimes best understood in terms of the separation of content from the means of delivery (the conduit). This distinction between content and conduit forms the basis of chapter 13. The enhancements to media through place, purpose, and text are discussed in chapter 14, along with such other topics as time displacement and the importance of effort in the choice of communication media.

The myths of convergence of media and industries are discussed in chapter 15. Finally, chapter 16 examines the evolving structure of the communication industry.

11

Services

In this chapter, a number of communication services are described and analyzed using the taxonomy developed previously in part II of this book. This chapter shows how the taxonomy can be used to improve our understanding of communication media.

AUTODIALERS

Autodialers are used in telemarketing to call individual telephones and transmit a prerecorded message. Receiving a call from an automated autodialer is annoying to most people, and some states have attempted to outlaw their use.

Autodialers use the telephone network to broadcast advertisements. Table 11.1 compares media according to the directionality of the network (one-way or two-way) and the audience (one-to-many or one-to-one).

Autodialers use the telephone network, normally a one-to-one, two-way, switched network intended for interpersonal communication. Usually, this would not make much sense. Radio is a much less expensive way to reach many people with the same message. The telephone network and the Internet were not designed nor intended to be broadcast networks. However, autodialers force people to listen by interrupting the normal activities at home. Most people are annoyed by them and consider them an inappropriate use of the telephone network. The many advertisements that appear over the Internet are likewise annoying. All the e-mail advertisements, called *spam*, are likewise annoying. Software is available to recognize and delete them.

Table 11.1   Comparison of media according to directionality and audience.

DIRECTIONALITY OF NETWORK	AUDIENCE	
	one-to-many (broadcast)	one-to-one (interpersonal)
one-way	radio television	
two-way	autodialers	telephone

Call-blocking on the telephone network is one way to prevent autodialers and telemarketers from calling.

SILENT RADIO

Silent Radio was a service, initiated in California, that transmitted text during the invisible vertical retrace interval of a broadcast television signal. The text was decoded and displayed as a moving line of text. News, sports, and weather information were featured, along with advertisements. Silent Radio receivers were used in restaurants, banks, and other public places where people had time to spare to read the display.

Silent Radio is similar to teletext in that textual information of mass market appeal is delivered by telecommunication. Both services use the vertical retrace interval of the broadcast TV signal to carry the information. A screen of information consisting of a few dozen lines of text is displayed with teletext. Silent Radio displays only a single line of text in a moving format similar to the Times Square display. Teletext is interactive in the sense that the user can request a screen, or page, of information. Silent Radio is totally passive: the viewer can see the information only as it passes in display.

Both teletext and Silent Radio are electronic media, although their interactivity differ. Billboards are a paper-based passive medium; newspapers and magazines are also paper-based media, but they are interactive in the sense that the user turns pages as they are read.

TALKING NEWSPAPERS

The newspaper is a paper-based, print medium. Newspapers contain news, full-page advertisements, and classified advertisements. Newspapers are still physically delivered, although physical delivery is becoming increasingly costly. Furthermore, newsprint is costly, and the recycling of paper is some-thing of a chore for consumers. Years ago, some newspaper publishers believed that videotex—an electronic information service for the home, delivered over telephone lines and displayed on the home TV set—was the solution to these problems and could also create new opportunities for classified listings. How-ever, consumers did not respond favorably. The technology was costly and difficult to use. An alternative solution was the talking newspaper.

The talking newspaper requires a touchtone telephone to access a data-base. Some of its services are talking ads, classified listings, and real estate information. The talking newspaper is another example of the use of the tele-phone to access all sorts of information stored in computerized databases, a type of service generically known as audiotex. The talking newspaper was yet another attempt at developing an electronic newspaper.

THE ELECTRONIC NEWSPAPER

The newspaper as we know it is a paper-based print medium that is delivered physically to newsstands, homes, and vending machines. The production of newspapers frequently involves the electronic transmission of pictorial and text data from the news source to the printing location. Communication sat-ellites are usually used for national newspapers. But as far as the consumer is concerned, newspapers are delivered physically.

Prior to World War II, newspapers were delivered electronically to tens of thousands of homes using facsimile transmission over the telephone net-work. The introduction of television at the end of the war, however, made this early form of electronic newspaper obsolete. During the past years, facsimile became popular, particularly at most businesses. Some daily and weekly news-letters were delivered electronically by facsimile over the telephone network. These fax-papers are an interesting use of the telephone network as a means of broadcasting information to many recipients, even if on a one-by-one basis.

Teletext is another way to obtain news electronically as text. The news is broadcast over the air with the TV signal, and individual pages (called frames) of information are retrieved and displayed on the home TV screen. The TV set's remote control is used in an interactive fashion to specify the desired frame. The information contained in the teletext database is mostly timely, general-interest news. As was mentioned earlier, teletext is available in Europe, but not in the United States.

Videotex was initially promoted to the consumer as the electronic newspaper of the future. The newspaper companies that became involved with videotex did so because of concerns over the rising costs of paper, the increasing difficulties in obtaining people willing to deliver newspapers to homes every day, and the need to protect their lucrative classified listings. But very few consumers subscribed to videotex.

What was discovered was that the few consumers that subscribed did not use videotex as an electronic newspaper but rather as a form of interpersonal communication, or electronic mail. Today's great success of the Internet for e-mail thus is no surprise. Perhaps videotex and its vast database of information were too complicated for most people to comprehend. The success of the search engines and browsers of the Internet and the World Wide Web make the searching and accessing of information relatively simple.

Audiotex is the use of a touchtone telephone to request information from a database. The information is returned in the form of synthesized speech. Audiotex is used to access all sorts of newslike information—a type of service known as "talking newspapers." Audiotex offers on-demand access to specific and general-interest information.

Table 11.2 compares the various electronic media for obtaining news using the text and speech modalities.

Another way to characterize electronic access to news is whether the information is broadcast to many recipients or whether specific desired information can be obtained on demand. Text is usually accessed on demand in such services as videotex, teletext, and the World Wide Web. Speech as a modality can be broadcast as in AM/FM radio or on demand as in audiotex.

The success of teletext indicates that consumers want some information immediately, on demand. The problem with obtaining news over AM and FM radio is that the listener must wait until the desired information is sent; AM

Table 11.2. The means of distribution for various media for different modalities.

MODALITY	DISTRIBUTION	
	Broadcast	Switched
Text	teletext	fax-newspapers
		videotex
		World Wide Web
Speech	AM/FM radio	audiotex

and FM radio are fine for listening to news when specific facts are not desired. It is frustrating to be listening to the car radio hoping to soon hear whether the Holland or the Lincoln Tunnel is less crowded when a commuter is already on his or her way into New York City. An audiotex service containing traffic information that could be accessed over a cellular car telephone would seem to me to have good prospects for success for traffic information.

Facsimile seems to be well suited for electronic newspapers. However, the telephone network really was not designed for the broadcasting of information to many facsimile terminals. A better way might seem to be the use of some of the spare capacity of an FM radio station or the vertical retrace interval of a broadcast TV signal. The broadcast signal could be received by a special decoder and then converted for use by the facsimile terminal. But transmitting news by radio fax was tried decades ago and failed.

There are a number of interesting and novel possibilities for the electronic distribution of newspapers and news to augment the conventional paper-based newspaper and perhaps someday replace them altogether. Many newspapers have embraced the Internet and offer their content on the World Wide Web. Many are free for today's news but charge for older articles from their archives. However, today's paper-based newspaper and other media still seem to have a future, since we still seem to have an insatiable appetite for paper.

TALKING BOOKS

During the past few years, books recorded on audiocassettes have become quite popular and are sold in bookstores. The basic idea of a "talking book" is actually quite old, and books were recorded for the blind decades ago. Today's talking books are listened to during the daily commute in the car or on the subway. The reading of a newspaper on the train has been replaced for many by listening to a talking book. Talking books are an interesting example of a modality crossover from one medium to another.

EDUCATIONAL TECHNOLOGY

Much of education is communication. A textbook is a printed communication medium. The teacher in front of the classroom is a form of interpersonal communication, although it frequently is more one-way and passive than it should be. One advantage of the computer when used in education is that it actively involves the participation of the student, avoiding the passivity of the classroom.

Communication technology can help mediate education over distance. The class can be regarded as a meeting, and thus telemeeting and teleconferencing are applicable to education. A variety of telecommunication technologies ranging from simple audio-only to full-motion one-way video with audio return can be used in education to extend the classroom to distant locations, and such technologies have been used for decades by engineering schools in the United States. A course can also be recorded on a videocassette and physically delivered to a distant location. Questions can be telephoned to the instructor or can be sent by facsimile or electronic mail.

The use of television in education is still consistently passive, and ways are needed to increase the active involvement of students. One way might be a videocassette that can be stopped for questions and comments with a teaching assistant operating the VCR and being available to stimulate questions and discussions. Another way might be to interrupt the flow of the video lecture and ask the student to think about the material just covered. In this regard, the interactive digital video disc might be particularly helpful, although a properly prepared videotape might serve just as well.

The Internet is yet another way to deliver education over distance. Some universities are convinced that students will complete their degree program over the Web. Yet many students prefer the conventional classroom. There has always been a market for distance education for students who cannot attend conventional classes. Correspondence schools use conventional mail to deliver education and return the graded work of the distant students. The Internet seems to be really little more than a more technologically advanced form of correspondence education—albeit more interactive and media rich.

MASS MEDIA: THE TELEPHONE

The telephone is an interpersonal communication medium that is used mostly for one-on-one telecommunication. The telephone is not considered a mass medium for broadcasting information to many recipients, but with new technology, the telephone is extending its traditional boundary and is becoming a medium for mass communication. Two examples will demonstrate these mass uses of the telephone. The first example is the 900 service that enables the caller to reach a small number of other callers for a group conference call. This service is called a chat line.

The second example is the use of automatic programmable dialers that call many people one by one and play a prerecorded message. The message usually is a sales pitch, and this type of "junk call" is very annoying to some people. In this example, the telephone is being used as a broadcast communication medium, although the message is broadcast nonsimultaneously to the recipients.

PAGERS

Paging appears in old movies when an attendant walks through the lobby calling "Paging Mr. Smith!" Everyone hears the message, but only Mr. Smith responds. The basic concept of paging is that the paging call is sent to everyone, but only the intended recipient responds. Wireless radio pagers perform in the same way. The wireless paging signal is transmitted by radio waves and received by all paging units, but only the pager of the intended recipient displays the transmitted paging message.

Early wireless pagers displayed only the telephone number of the person who was issuing the page. Today's units now display also the name of the person initiating the page. Pagers also can display short text messages. Used this way, pagers are a form of wireless electronic mail. The Internet is used for paging when an instant message is sent in the form of text to another person, who can then reply immediately. Various conduits for paging using different modalities are shown in table 11.3.

Table 11.3. Examples of different paging services using various conduits and modalities.

CONDUIT	SERVICE	MODALITY
physical	voice paging	speech
wireless	wireless pagers	text
Internet	instant messaging	text
	chat rooms	

12

Computer Communication

The digital computer is a powerful machine for performing calculations and other operations under the control of a stored program. Word processing and spreadsheet analyses are only two examples of some of the many useful applications of a personal digital computer. When equipped with a modem, a personal computer becomes a communication device to access the World Wide Web through the Internet. This chapter discusses the use of a computer for communication and also describes how people communicate with a computer.

HUMAN-MACHINE COMMUNICATION

People communicate with a computer through various modalities, such as by text typed on keyboards, by visual displays, and by speech. Language, either in the form of text or as spoken speech, is the most natural form of communication for people, but computers have their own language—digital bits—that is far from natural for most people. Icons and pull-down menus are part of the graphic user interface to make communication with a computer easy and natural for people and yet be compatible with the computer.

Researchers have developed the technology to allow computers to understand spoken speech and to generate understandable synthetic speech, but near-perfect performance is still elusive. Typed text, a mouse, and a visual display are the easiest ways for most people to communicate with computers. But there is a fascination with machines that are human in most ways, including an ability to respond to spoken speech and to speak in natural-sounding

Table 12.1.   Various input and output technologies for human/computer communication using different modalities.

| | MODALITY | | |
	Text/Graphics	Speech	Touch
Input	keyboard mouse	speech recognition	mouse joystick touch screen
Output	display	speech synthesis	"feelie" device

synthetic speech. Table 12.1 gives the various modalities of communication between people and computers for input to the computer and output from it.

Computer-generated graphical imagery superimposed over real images coupled with the tactual sensation of a "feelie" device can create a form of virtual reality. A computer-generated virtual reality could be a new medium of communication between humans and computers. But most human-computer communication is more mundane, using simple keyboards and displays of text. For interpersonal electronic telecommunication by speech, the telephone is the medium of choice. Text in the form of e-mail can also be used for interpersonal electronic telecommunication. Speech synthesis and speech recognition can be used for human-computer communication, but its use is limited thus far, other than for those who are visually impaired.

Clearly, text and point-and-click with a mouse are the modalities of choice for interactive communication between a person and a computer, and speech is the modality of choice for interactive communication between people.

The mouse, icons, and pull-down menus are very friendly ways of communication between people and computers, as demonstrated decades ago by the success of the Apple Macintosh computer. Touch is not yet an extensive form of communication between people and computers, other than touch screens. Computers also communicate directly with other computers through the exchange of data in the form of bits.

COMPUTER TELECOMMUNICATION

Internet-based services, such as e-mail, electronic banking, home information, and e-commerce, use a computer as a terminal for text and graphic telecommunication to obtain and exchange information. The remainder of this chapter treats these applications, including the use of the Internet and the World Wide Web.

When used for communication, a computer is a terminal for communication based on text and graphics. One application is communication with another terminal—e-mail—a form of interpersonal communication. Although many people might believe e-mail is relatively new, the use of text as a form of electronic communication is as old as the electric telegraph of 150 years ago.

With e-mail, text messages are composed and transmitted to a distant computer for later reading by a specific person or a group of persons. Electronic bulletin boards are text-based e-mail systems accessed and read by a number of users. Chat lines and instant messaging facilitate direct connection between computers as terminals to allow people to communicate immediately and interactively through text messages. Teletypewriter machines have been used for decades by people who are hearing impaired to communicate by text over the telephone network.

A second application of communication by computer is to reach a second computer to cause a transaction to occur. With home banking, funds are transferred using a personal computer to instruct the bank's computer to cause the appropriate transaction to occur.

A third application of communication by computer is to retrieve information stored in databases—a major use of the Internet and the World Wide Web. The information stored in the databases can be of a specialized nature or of a general-interest nature. Text and graphical information is retrieved from these databases.

The three applications for computer communication are

- interpersonal (terminal-to-terminal),
- transaction (terminal-to-computer), and
- information retrieval (terminal-to-database)
  - specialized information
  - general-interest information.

The technological requirements for these three applications are compared in table 12.2.

This chart implies that the retrieval of general-interest information is different in technical requirements compared to other forms of computer

Table 12.2. Technological requirements for different applications of computer communications.

	INTERACTION	CONTENT	KEYBOARD
• Interpersonal	two-way	text	alphanumeric
• Transaction	two-way	text	alphanumeric
• Information:			
- specialized	two-way	text & graphics	alphanumeric
- general	limited selection	text & graphics	numeric

communication. Interpersonal communication, transactions, and much specialized information retrieval all appear to share similar requirements: a terminal that displays mostly text and has an alphanumeric keyboard. These requirements describe the French Minitel terminal. These requirements also describe much of the Internet and World Wide Web.

Information retrieval of broad, general-interest information benefits from graphics, in color, along with text. However, the limited selection and content of general-interest information implies that only a keypad is needed to select the desired frame of information. These requirements describe teletext.

The segmentation of computer communication into these two general areas is made even clearer when the marketing aspects of the three types of computer communication are considered. The marketing aspects considered in table 12.3 are the appeal and advantages to the consumer, the positioning of the product and service, and the market potential.

What emerges from these charts and analyses is that there seem to be two quite different types of computer-communication services. The need to access timely, general-interest information in an on-demand manner seems quite distinct from the other types of computer communication. The need to access general-interest information is most effectively solved through tele-text—hence its success in Europe. Some form of very simple—perhaps wire-less—terminal might also be appropriate for this type of information.

VIDEOTEX

Remote display terminals with keyboards have been used for many decades to access information stored in computerized data banks or databases. The information was highly specialized, such as the legal information stored in the LEXIS system or the abstracts of medical articles stored in the MED-LINE system. The airlines developed very large database systems for airline

Table 12.3.   Marketing position and network implications for computer communications.

	APPEAL	POSITIONING	MARKET
• Interpersonal	save time & money	home communication & work center	mass
• Transaction	increase efficiency	home communication & work center	mass
• Information:			
- specialized	utilitarian	home work center	limited
- general	fast, easy access	home entertainment center	mass

	NETWORK	
• Interpersonal	two-way switched	telephone network
• Transaction	two-way switched	data network
• Information:		
- specialized	two-way switched	data network
- general	two-way one-way with selection	data network broadcast network

reservations, such as United Airlines' Apollo system and American Airlines' Sabre system.

As computers came to be used in homes by hobbyists and others, database services for the home were developed, such as CompuServe and The Source. The home user simply connected a modem (short for *modulator-demodulator*) to a telephone line and placed a telephone call to the remote database. These home services were used mostly to post and to send messages to other users, an early form of e-mail.

In the late 1970s, the British Post Office started work on a centralized database service intended for home users. The British recognized that such a home information service would need to be easy to use and inexpensive. Ease of use was achieved by organizing the information in the database in a tree fashion so that the user could slowly and methodically search for the desired information. The cost of the terminal, which connected to a telephone line, was kept low by using the home TV set to display the information. The service was also made "friendly" through the use of color and simple graphics. The British launched their service around 1980 after spending about $50 million in its development; it was called Prestel viewdata service. Later, the term *videotex* was used to apply to such database services for the home. The British expected Prestel to achieve a mass market. It did not; by mid-1984, only about seventeen thousand Prestel terminals were in British homes.

In 1983, AT&T and the Knight-Ridder Newspapers launched a videotex service, called Viewtron service, in southeastern Florida. It too failed to achieve significant consumer acceptance and was closed down a few years later. A videotex service launched in Southern California by AT&T and Times-Mirror also closed after a few years. In 1989, IBM and Sears launched their own videotex service, called Prodigy service, after spending more than $500 million in its development. But Prodigy had a very difficult time recovering its initial investment and its yearly operating costs.

The French made a national commitment to their version of videotex, called Télétel. A terminal, called Minitel, with a monochrome display, alphanumeric keyboard, and telephone was developed and supplied for free to French telephone subscribers. The database contains listings of all telephone numbers, and a major use of the Télétel system is to obtain telephone numbers. Another frequent use is to send personal messages to other users—a form of electronic mail. Years ago, millions of Minitel terminals were in use in French homes and businesses. In terms of implementation, Minitel was a success. However, the cost of that success was quite high, and a 1989 study by the French government accounting office concluded the service had lost a large sum of money. A considerable amount of French pride was involved in achieving technological leadership in what the French call *infomatique*. But the rest of the world embraced the Internet and the protocols of the World Wide Web. Today, the Internet and the World Wide Web are used extensively in France too.

HOME INFORMATION

The use of a terminal in the home to access databases and other services is called *home information*. The British videotex approach met with poor consumer acceptance, seeming to imply that the use of the home TV set to display e-mail, transactions, and specialized information was a serious deficiency. The Internet is accessed mostly through the use of a personal computer with its own dedicated display.

The Source and CompuServe were two of the first home information services in the United States. However, these systems were text-based, and keywords were used to search for information in the database, which was then displayed line by line. The shared use of a computerized database was called

Table 12.4. Distinguishing characteristics of various home information services.

	VIDEOTEX	INTERNET/WWW	TELETEXT
Modality	text & graphics	text & graphics	text & graphics
Form	color	B&W & color	color
Organization	tree organized	search organized	frame oriented
Display	home TV	personal computer	home TV
Database	centralized	decentralized	centralized
Size	large	large	small
Content	information access	messaging	timely
		information access	general interest
			on demand

online access. The term *videotex* became corrupted and extended to include all viewdata-like and online services. The term *videotex* is no longer used.

Videotex and online systems for the home failed in most countries. The British Prestel videotex service was a mass market failure, as was the German Bildshirmtext service. The Source and CompuServe had subscribers numbering in the hundreds of thousands in the United States as did the Prodigy videotex service owned by IBM and Sears. However, many of the users of these services were computer hobbyists or other users who sent personal messages to other users. The services were also used to access stock-price information. They all were difficult to use for the untrained user. A personal computer, a modem, and specialized computer programs were required to use them. Table 12.4 lists the distinguishing characteristics of videotex, the Internet (World Wide Web), and teletext.

Teletext is a relatively simple system, which contributed greatly to its former success. Other forms of computer communication for home information are more complex and involve a number of ingredients.

INGREDIENTS

Computer telecommunication involves some major components or ingredients. First, a terminal is required. This could be a personal computer with a modem for telecommunication and appropriate computer programs, or software. Next, a telecommunication network is required. This could be the ubiquitous telephone network or some form of specialized data-communication network, such as the packet-switched Internet. If the terminal were being used to send messages to another terminal, such as with e-mail, this is all that would be needed, although a centrally located host computer makes universal access easier.

The terminal could also be used to access a centrally located computer to cause some transaction to occur or to access a centrally located database to extract some information. In these two applications, the centrally located computer or database would definitely be required, along with appropriate software. For the consumer market, the software would need to be particularly easy to use, or user-friendly. If financial transactions are being performed from the terminal, the issue of computer security arises. It is essential that a user not be able to use a terminal to gain unauthorized access to some computer system or some files.

Thus, computer communication is a complex system involving the interconnection and interaction of a number of hardware and software components. The French Télétel system achieved significant market penetration in France years ago through the use of a relatively inexpensive and unsophisticated terminal and also through control and specification of the total system. The Internet and World Wide Web of today have achieved considerable acceptance and growth by following similar philosophies of ease of use and universal standards.

THE INTERNET AND THE WORLD WIDE WEB

Videotex failed around the world. But in the 1990s, the Internet and the World Wide Web achieved consumer acceptance and use, along with impressive growth. How could one fail and the other succeed so dramatically? Table 12.5 compares videotex and access to the World Wide Web over the Internet.

The characteristics that differ between videotex and the Internet/Web could be very significant in explaining the failure of videotex and the success of the Internet/Web. Videotex used the home TV set for display. This created many problems, one being conflict between TV viewing and use of the TV for display of information. Furthermore, the home TV set is positioned as a central component for entertainment—not information seeking and messaging. The use of a centralized database, organized in a tree fashion, was difficult to search through to find information. The Internet/Web consists of many databases, all decentralized and disorganized. Search engines and a common format for data storage and retrieval make the overall system transparent and easy to use.

Table 12.5. Comparison of videotex and the Internet.

	VIDEOTEX	INTERNET/WEB
Terminal	keyboard adapter	personal computer
Display Device	TV set	dedicated CRT
Keyboard	alphanumeric	alphanumeric
Display Specs	low resolution	high resolution
	color	color
	text & graphics	text & graphics
Access	modem & phone line	modem & phone line
Messaging	rudimentary e-mail	e-mail
Database	centralized	decentralized
	tree organized	disorganized
Positioning	home entertainment center	home work center
	FAILURE	SUCCESS

WebTV is a terminal for accessing the Internet/Web using the home TV set for display. In this respect, WebTV is similar to videotex. Thus far, even though well over a few years old, WebTV has been poorly accepted by consumers. This would seem to confirm that the real problem with videotex was the use of the home TV set for display.

The Internet is a data network interconnecting computers around the world. The data network uses packet switching, which is very efficient for the short bursts of data that characterize most computer telecommunication. The World Wide Web is an overall concept for information retrieval based on the use of a standardized format, called *hypertext markup language (HTML)*, and browser software to display the retrieved information in a friendly, easy-to-use manner. Search engines catalogue all the various sites accessible over the Internet so that users can search for almost any topic in a disorganized fashion—and find it, along with all sorts of unwanted information too.

AUDIOTEX

A display terminal is needed to access the Internet for information. But some of the need for custom, individualized information can be served by audiotex.

Audiotex uses a standard touchtone telephone and the telephone network. Touchtone keys are pressed in response to audio prompts to the user. The desired information is in the form of synthetic and recorded speech. Audiotex is used by many banks to enable customers to verify account balances, deposits, and payments. Audiotex is used by airlines so that people can call and verify flight arrival and departure times. Audiotex is being used at many universities to allow students to register for courses from home. Audiotex is easy to use, friendly, and as ubiquitous as a touchtone telephone. But its appeal has become limited because of the widespread availability of personal computers and Internet access.

It can take much time to listen to a large amount of information. Usually it is much faster to read large amounts of information from a screen. For these applications, the use of text makes much more sense. Hence, the success of the Internet and the World Wide Web. But when walking or when driving an automobile, it is unsafe and difficult to also read information from the display of a cell phone or the screen of a personal digital assistant (PDA). For cell phones and wireless PDAs, one way to access information is audio, using speech recognition of spoken commands and requests for information with the requested information presented as synthesized speech.

WIRELESS INTERNET

The use of wireless PDAs to access information over the Internet is known as the *wireless Internet*. But this is not the only application of wireless technology to access information when a person is on the move.

The cellular telephone was initially intended for use in automobiles. These early large and bulky wireless telephones have evolved into today's highly miniaturized cell phones, which are carried in pockets and purses. The Global Positioning System (GPS) uses communication satellites to determine a location precisely, and this GPS position then enables mapping software to show the position on a map display. Some automobiles have this GPS mapping system already installed. Verbal driving instructions guide the driver to the final destination. Will this application diffuse to wireless PDAs and cell phones, using speech both for input and for output of information? Or is it easier to read information on a small screen on the cell phone and PDA?

HOME BANKING

Virtually every major bank in the United States has been at some time involved in home banking. Home banking initially meant the use of a videotex-like terminal to access bank computers for the purpose of paying bills, verifying account balances, and performing other banking transactions.

Home banking was sometimes packaged with other videotex services. The consumer response was very disappointing, and many of the home banking services were quietly withdrawn. Most of these home banking systems were much more trouble to use than they were worth. Also, most consumers have a real need for cash, but no home terminal has thus far solved the cash-dispensing problem.

Although the cash-dispensing home terminal never developed, many people do use their personal computers to access the Internet to perform various financial transactions. Goods are purchased, stock prices examined, financial securities purchased, and funds transferred between different accounts. Encryption assures the security of these Internet transactions.

CD-ROM

There may be a need for access to large databases of specialized information that do not change frequently with time. Such databases are stored digitally on small read-only discs, similar in size to the compact discs used in audio. Such discs are called *CD-ROMs*, for *compact disc read-only memory*. CD-ROMs are used to store encyclopedias, dictionaries, and large catalogues. The CD-ROMs are read by appropriate drives attached to personal computers. The CD-ROMs are physically delivered. Their information content is mostly text, but graphics and even moving images can also be stored on them. A key issue is whether most consumers have a need at home to access the information that can be stored in such large databases. Another issue is the difficulty in searching the database to find the desired information. Also, reading large amounts of information from a computer screen can be a tiresome chore. Paper will not disappear anytime in the near future.

REFERENCES

Noll, A. Michael. "Teletext and Videotex in North America: Service and System Implications." *Telecommunications Policy* 4, no. 1 (March 1980): 17–24.

———. "Videotex: Anatomy of a Failure." *Information & Management* 9, no. 2 (September 1985): 99–109.

Sigel, Efrem, ed. *Videotext: The Coming Revolution in Home/Office Information Retrieval.* New York: Harmony Books, 1980.

Tydeman, John, et. al. *Teletext and Videotex in the United States.* New York: McGraw Hill, 1982.

13

Content and Conduits

A communication conduit is the communication channel (or medium) that carries the content (or message). The telephone network, consisting of a variety of transmission media, is the conduit for speech, facsimile, and data. The telephone companies that own the conduit are considered common carriers and exercise no control over the content carried over their networks. Compact discs are the conduit for music and other audio programming. Newspapers are a conduit for text and the articles written by the reporters. Coaxial cable is the conduit for cable television. Cable television companies control both the conduit and the content. The relationship between content and conduit can help in understanding some policy issues involving cable television.

CATV: CONTENT, CONDUIT, OR BOTH?

The moving imagery of the video program is the content of television. The imagery can be delivered to the home over a variety of conduits. Some television conduits involve physical delivery, such as videotapes and DVDs rented from the video store. Other television conduits involve over-the-air transmission, such as VHF and UHF broadcasting and direct broadcast satellites (DBS), and transmission over coaxial cable and optical fiber, such as CATV broadcasting.

A single television broadcaster (such as the local affiliated station of the major networks ABC, CBS, NBC, and Fox in the United States) controls a single broadcast television channel in the VHF and UHF radio spectrum. The broadcaster determines the content that is carried over this channel, but no single broadcaster controls all the VHF and UHF spectrum space. Since spectrum space is a scarce resource, the Federal Communications Commission regulates and controls its allocation.

Competition characterizes television that is delivered over a variety of media. For example, there are a number of VHF and UHF stations competing with each other, along with direct broadcast satellite TV. Also, there are a number of video stores competing with each other in the rental and sale of videotapes. Since competition exists in the provision of television programming to the home, cable television claims it should be immune from regulation.

Over-the-air broadcasting and video stores are conduits, and there clearly is competition within each conduit in terms of independent sources of video programming. The coaxial cable of the CATV firm is the conduit, and there is only one coax to the home. The CATV company—the owner of the single conduit—determines and dictates the content carried over the coaxial cable. At one time there were three DBS providers, but that number is dwindling as DBS moves toward a similar monopoly status as CATV. The various contents and conduits for television are shown in table 13.1.

What this analysis suggests is that the ownership of the conduit should perhaps be separated from the control and packaging of the content carried over the coaxial cable. In essence, CATV could then be more like the provision of telephone service in which the ownership of the conduit—the telephone network—is fully separate from the content carried over the conduit. The CATV firm that owned and operated the coaxial cable would then be a common carrier. Channel space on the cable would be sold openly to various content providers and/or viewers, who would pay to watch various television shows.

Yet another model for the delivery of television is the use of a two-way, switched network to enable consumers to request and download individual

Table 13.1. The conduit control, and competition within it, for various video programming sources.

CONDUIT	CONTROL	CONDUIT COMPETITION
VHF/UHF spectrum	broadcasters	yes
videotape	video stores	yes
satellite	DBS providers	very little
coaxial cable	CATV firm	no

video content. This kind of switched video was known as *video dial tone (VDT)* or *video on demand (VOD)*. Many of the systems used optical fiber as the conduit, either direct to the home (called *fiber to the home, FTTH*) or to the curb or neighborhood of the homes of the users. Telephone companies and some media firms investigated such switched video during the 1990s, but consumers were not interested. The same model has appeared again, but with delivery over the packet-switched Internet—a service known as *Internet-protocol television (IPTV)*. But the high-speed bandwidth needed to carry separate video programs, even when compressed, to millions of homes would be very costly and complex.

Over-the-air broadcast television requires a considerable amount of radio spectrum space. That space could perhaps be better used for interpersonal communication, such as mobile telephone service. Cable television has achieved impressive market penetration in the United States, and presently CATV passes about 98 percent of TV households, and about 64 percent of TV households subscribe to CATV. In 2001, only about 13 percent of households in the United States obtained their television solely from over-the-air VHF and UHF broadcasting.

Since CATV passes nearly all TV households in the United States, with nearly two-thirds subscribing, and with the percentage of over-the-air households dwindling, perhaps the continued broadcasting of television over the air no longer makes much sense. As national policy, CATV and DBS perhaps should be required to connect to every TV household and provide basic over-the-air television for free. The broadcast TV networks might pay the CATV firm for access to viewers, or alternatively the CATV firm might pay the broadcaster for the right to retransmit the video programming. A fund to subsidize the provision of over-the-air television might be created. Although the solutions might not be clear, it is clear that over-the-air broadcast television and CATV are going to experience much change and policy discussion over the next decade. Perhaps the distinction presented here between content and conduit might help focus that debate.

VIDEO PROGRESSION

Moving images are the content of motion pictures. These moving images are carried over a variety of conduits: broadcast VHF and UHF over-the-air television, DBS, CATV, videotapes, and digital video discs (DVDs).

Movies are distributed to the various conduits in a well-planned progression. They are first released to motion picture theaters. After a few months, a movie is then released for sale on videotape and DVD. It will then be shown over pay channels on CATV and DBS. Next, the movie is released for rental on videotape. Finally, the movie will be shown on VHF networks and local television. Along the way, the movie will also be shown on airlines. This progression of the same content through a variety of conduits has been carefully planned and timed to maximize profits to all the various involved parties.

AUDIO PROGRESSION

Different forms of recorded audio media have found their own individual markets depending upon content. This is a new trend compared to the days of the 78 rpm, twelve-inch record, which was used for classical, popular, and other content. The long-playing 33⅓ rpm record was used for classical music and for collections of popular songs and of rock numbers. The smaller-diameter 45 rpm record was initially used for classical music, in addition to other content, but the LP ultimately displaced this use. The 45 found its own unique market for single popular songs and rock numbers: the 45 single.

The audiocassette is used for classical, popular, and rock content. It is used mostly in the automobile and in small, portable tape machines, such as the Sony Walkman machine. The audiocassette has coexisted with the LP and 45 records. The compact disc (CD) has totally displaced the 33⅓ LP record for all forms of music. One wonders what has happened to the cassingle for pop/rock singles. The cassingle was an audiocassette that contained only a single short piece of music. A small three-inch-diameter CD, which held about fifteen minutes of content, was introduced to the market in the late 1980s. It could have been a replacement for the 45 and the cassingle, but it was too costly for the teenagers who purchase singles.

Table 13.2. Progression of audio media.

CONTENT	PAST	PRESENT	FUTURE
classical	LP & cassette	CD	?
pop/rock:			
albums	LP & cassette	CD	MP3 & compression
singles	45 & cassingle	CD	MP3 & compression

Classical music led the revolution of the digital compact disc, and pop music followed. Today, pop music is leading the revolution of the compressed digital format of MP3 through the downloading of pop music over the Internet, although serious copyright and ownership issues have appeared. Pieces of pop music are relatively short, so that an MP3 file is manageable. Many classical music compositions are an hour or so in length, and thus the MP3 format is still bulky to download with today's technology. Compression technology continues to improve, the capacity and cost of solid-state storage continues to decline, and the revolution of a world of solid-state music storage with no moving media has already started.

PHYSICAL DELIVERY

A number of communication media are delivered physically. Such recorded media as videotapes and compact discs are delivered physically. Letters are delivered by post. The daily newspaper is physically delivered to the home, to the newsstand, and to the newspaper vending machine. Physical transportation is a major component in the delivery of many communication media.

Even electronically delivered media frequently involve physical delivery. Consider placing a telephone call or using the Internet to purchase an item. The ultimate delivery of the purchased item is by truck to the home. Although placing the order is performed electronically, the final satisfaction comes with the arrival of the physically delivered goods.

The need to deliver large documents and other material quickly has resulted in a booming overnight air-delivery business. Vast amounts of information are contained in many media that can be delivered physically, such as DVDs, compact discs, computer disks, and even paper-based reports. Physical delivery, even overnight express delivery, is relatively inexpensive and is an efficient way to deliver the message when instantaneous delivery by electronic telecommunication is not essential.

There is still a need for humans to drive the vehicles that deliver the goods. Automated physical delivery clearly could be the ultimate solution. Pneumatic tubes used to be popular in stores of the past and still are in use today: some airlines use them to deliver cash from the ticket counter to a central depository. Small tracked vehicles cart mail in large office buildings. Automated mail carts travel along routes marked invisibly on the carpets and floors of office buildings. Although automated physical delivery exists within buildings, it does not exist between buildings and cities. We still rely on such human-operated vehicles as trucks, vans, trains, boats, and airplanes. One wonders whether some system of automated physical delivery will someday be developed between cities, at least for small packages.

INFORMATION ACCESS AND DISSEMINATION

We saw that Shannon's model of the communication process included an information source and an information receiver. We will elaborate upon this model for the case of a human receiver or seeker of information.

There are two cases of interest. In the first case, the person is seeking information. The information might be some specific fact, such as the population of the United States or the schedule for the local movie theater. The information being sought could also be more extensive, such as a history of opera or an analysis of the financial performance of a company. The essential aspect of this case is that the seeker of information knows what information is being sought and is actively seeking it.

In the second case, information is being disseminated to people who are not actively seeking an answer to a specific question. The recipient of the information is passive. Some examples of these two cases might help illuminate them.

Consider a person who wants to know whether Beethoven's opera *Fidelio* is being performed next week at the San Francisco Opera. The person could telephone the opera house, use the Internet, or search through the local newspaper to obtain the answer. The person is an active seeker of information. Another example of active information seeking would be someone who wants to know tomorrow's weather forecast. The person could listen to the radio and wait until the forecast was made, could use the Internet, could search through the daily newspaper, or could phone the weather service. A variety of communication media are used in the process of seeking information, such as the telephone, newspapers, teletext, radio, television, and the Internet. It is not the medium used that is essential, but rather the intent of the user seeking information.

Many people read the newspaper as an entertaining way to be informed. This is an example of information that is disseminated, and the recipient is

Table 13.3. Sources of active and passive information.

MODALITY	INFORMATION SEEKING (active)	INFORMATION DISSEMINATION (passive)
audio	telephone	broadcast radio
text	encyclopedia	newspapers
	e-mail/Internet	magazines
images	teletext	television
	facsimile	movies

not actively seeking specific information. Again, a variety of media are used to disseminate information, such as radio, television, and newspapers.

Some media are more appropriate to information seeking, and other media are more appropriate to information dissemination, although most can be used in both cases. Table 13.3 attempts to categorize communication media according to these two cases.

14

Enhancements

The sensory appeal of entertainment media has been increasing over the years. For example, the addition of color was an increase in sensory appeal compared to monochrome television, and the stereo compact disc was a considerable increase in sensory appeal in terms of sound quality compared with old 78 rpm records.

The functionality of interpersonal communication media has likewise increased over time. Cellular wireless service, call forwarding, and answering machines all increase the functionality of telephone communication.

These increases in sensory appeal and in functionality are enhancements of the original medium. Color television is still the broadcast of moving images for entertainment purposes, and cellular wireless is simply plain old telephone service (POTS) while the user is mobile. The basic communication medium has not changed; it simply has been enhanced. Table 14.1 shows examples of some basic and enhanced communication media.

This chapter explores examples of enhancements of communication media and also the targeting of different media to different audiences. The displacement of time that occurred with videotapes is also discussed. The chapter ends with the presentation of a theory of effort in the choice of communication media.

PLACE ENHANCEMENT

During their early years, most communication media were available only at public places. A person had to take a letter to a public post office and return to

Table 14.1.   Examples of enhancements of media.

MEDIUM	BASIC	ENHANCED
Entertainment:		
• recorded audio	78 rpm record	digital CD
• moving images	monochrome TV	color TV & HDTV
Interpersonal:		
• speech	plain old telephone service	cellular wireless

retrieve any mail. The telegraph was available only in public telegraph offices. Most entertainment media were available initially at public places only, for example, the movie theater.

Place enhancement occurs when a communication medium is available not only at public places but also at home and other places. Television and the VCR brought movies from the motion picture theater into the home. E-mail brings telegraphy into the home and office. Mail deliveries are made directly to the home, although at a much less frequent schedule than decades ago when two deliveries a day were the norm. Audio recordings bring the concert hall into the home.

Place enhancement usually does not replace an older medium. Television has not replaced the motion picture theater; audio recordings have not replaced the concert hall; and e-mail and the telephone have not displaced the handwritten letter.

PURPOSE ENHANCEMENT

In the world of text, newspapers primarily inform the reader about world and local events. Newspapers have been enhanced through the use of pictures, graphics, and color. This enhances newspapers by improving and extending their value to entertain. Television is primarily an entertainment medium. The use of news on television enhances television by giving it an additional purpose: namely, to inform. Figure 14.1 shows these enhancements by purpose.

TEXT ENHANCEMENT

Text can be added to communication media to enhance their use. One example of this is the use of text with the telephone to identify the telephone number of the calling party—a service known as *caller ID*. Another example is

MODALITY	ENTERTAIN	enhancement	INFORM
text	X	⟵ ▭ • pictures • graphics • color	NEWSPAPERS
moving images	TELEVISION	▭ ⟹ • news	X

FIGURE 14.1
Examples of enhancements in purpose for different modalities

teletext, which can be used to give listings for television programs. Another example would be the use of a single-line text display to give program information when listening to the radio. The use of text to enhance electronically delivered communication media is depicted in table 14.2.

AUDIENCE PARTICIPATION

The audience for many mass media has changed over time. Moving images were viewed in Edison's kinetoscope initially by individual persons. During its early days, watching television was a family affair. Today's small television receivers and video DVD machines with their built-in small-screen displays are intended for personal viewing—in essence, a return to yesterday's kinetoscope in terms of audience viewing behavior.

Motion pictures are viewed by large groups of people at movie theaters. The group experience of viewing a movie at the theater adds to the impact of the medium. The large screen, high-quality image, and impressive audio add

Table 14.2. Examples of the use of text to enhance electronically delivered media.

MODALITY	ENTERTAIN	ENHANCEMENT	INTERPERSONAL
sound	RADIO program identification	text	TELEPHONE caller identification
moving images	TELEVISION program identification	text	

Table 14.3. The audience for various media for different modalities of communication.

	AUDIENCE		
MODALITY	personal	small group	large group
moving images	kinetoscope video Walkman	television	movie theater
interpersonal	telephone	conference call speakerphone	teleconference
recorded audio	headphones	loudspeaker	discotheque

to the sensory appeal, but the shared experience of group viewing seems to be a major factor in attracting audiences to movie theaters.

During its earliest days, radio was listened to on a pair of headphones—a very personal form of individual participation. Later, the loudspeaker was added to radio receivers, and listening to the radio became a small group experience—usually a family affair. As radio receivers became less costly, many radios were found in the average home so that each person could listen to his or her favorite program. However, sound interference from one room to another was a problem, and the solution was a return to the use of headphones, or earphones. Recorded audio media, such as cassettes, compact discs, and MP3 audio, are also listened to on headphones for personal listening. Recorded audio is also listened to by large groups of people at discotheques.

The telephone always was primarily a personal form of communication. The telephone handset, which allows one to hear the other party's speech "whispering" directly into one's ear, creates a very intimate form of interpersonal telecommunication. The speakerphone allows a small group of people to telecommunicate, but the intimacy of the handset is missing. Teleconferencing enables small and large groups of people to telecommunicate.

Table 14.3 shows the audience for various communication media classified by modality.

TARGETING OF AUDIENCE

When broadcast radio was originally introduced by AT&T, it was used to transmit advertisements—a form of electronic yellow pages. Music was added to fill in the otherwise quiet periods between the ads. Today's broadcast radio and television media are promoted as entertainment media—not electronic advertising media.

Mass media can be targeted to specific audiences. Many magazines are very specialized in terms of the intended audience. *Seventeen* is targeted to teenage girls, *Dance Magazine* to dancers and people interested in ballet, *Popular Science* to the home handyperson. Network VHF television is very much a medium with a mass, general audience. CATV has many more channels and hence can afford to distribute programming targeted to specific audiences, such as MTV and CNN. Radio too has become more targeted, with music being broadcast primarily over FM stations and news and talk shows being broadcast over AM stations.

TIME DISPLACEMENT: VIDEOTAPES AND VIDEO ON DEMAND

The home videocassette recorder (VCR) has a number of uses. It can be used to play VCR tapes rented or purchased from the local video store. Used this way, the VCR brings us video entertainment whenever we want to watch it. However, there is a need to obtain the videotape, and in the case of rentals, this means a trip to the local video store. However, in some parts of the United States, the local pizza delivery store will deliver a videotape along with the pizza.

CATV is the video medium that brings video programming into most homes in the United States. Conventional VHF network shows, movies, all-news channels, and music videos are all available over cable. However, the shows must be watched when they are broadcast rather than at the viewer's convenience. The VCR solves this problem through time displacement. Such time displacement is also obtained with the use of digital storage within the TV set or CATV converter box. The TV show is converted to a compressed digital format and stored on a digital hard drive so that it can be retrieved and watched at leisure. Commercials can even be stripped. Another solution is video on demand.

With video on demand, the user would request a particular video program for viewing at any requested time. The requested video would then be sent over a dedicated channel to the home. Clearly, with many homes all requesting different programs for viewing at different times, considerable capacity is needed on the transmission medium to the home. The coaxial cable of CATV can carry as many as a few hundred channels, but this capacity would only serve a few hundred homes. Also, fairly sophisticated equipment would be needed at the CATV source to store and play all the various video programs. Of course, we could rewire the United States with optical fiber whose tremendous capacity could easily handle thousands of TV signals so that we all could have video on demand. But who will do the rewiring: the CATV firm or the telephone company? But perhaps a bigger question is who will ultimately pay the great cost for this rewiring.

There is another way to solve the problem with TV scheduling. The solution would be to send the various programs available for viewing repetitively at staggered times. Again, the bandwidth for all these additional transmissions becomes a problem, but with digital bandwidth compression, it may be possible to send about eight television signals in the space of one.

INTERNET TELEVISION

The continuing advances in bandwidth compression, particularly of television signals, might make it practical to transmit television over the packet-switched Internet—what is known as *Internet TV (ITV)* or also as *Internet protocol TV (IPTV)*. The use of the Internet—a switched medium—to convey television—a broadcast medium—is intriguing.

The use of the Internet to transmit television and video would be a natural progression from the use of the Internet to transmit radio programs to personal computers. Internet TV would be truly "video on demand," allowing consumers to download and stream video directly to their homes. But this will require some form of convergence between the television set and the personal computer—or digital processing and storage built into the TV set. It will also require vast amounts of transmission and switching capacity—far more than is available today or in the near future. Internet TV is still futuristic.

TIME DISPLACEMENT FOR RADIO

The audiocassette recorder can be used to record radio shows, but it lacks the automatic tuning and recording features of the VCR. If these features were added, then the audiocassette recorder could be programmed to record automatically specific radio shows at specific times. Radio, like television, could thus be time displaced too for listening at a later, more convenient time.

Drama shows used to be very popular on radio. Movies, soaps, situation comedies, and other programs on television have displaced radio for drama to a considerable extent. However, the sound of audio-only drama leaves much to the imagination of the listener and thus involves the listener in fantasy. The success of talking books on audiocassettes, though probably listened to in the car or on the subway train during the daily commute to and from work, implies that radio drama could have a renewed life. The one problem is that the shows might be broadcast at inconvenient times. Thus, some way to program an audio recorder could indeed be a key component in any hope for success with radio drama.

The solution to all this could be what is known as "podcasting." Various audio programs are downloaded to the personal computer in a compressed audio format and are then transferred to an iPod or other MP3 player for later listening.

EFFORT

Effort on the part of a human user is required to choose and to use a particular communication medium or modality. Some specific examples might help in understanding how effort impacts the choice and use of a communication medium.

Consider the choice between typing a short letter, making a telephone call, or using the Internet to obtain specific information. The typing of a letter requires a typewriter, or word processor, along with paper. The actual typing involves the movement of fingers along a keyboard. An envelope must then be addressed, the letter folded and inserted in it, and a stamp licked and placed on it. All these activities require some physical effort on the part of the letter writer. Most of this effort is eliminated with the Internet, however.

A telephone call requires only the dialing of a few digits. The message must then be spoken to the party at the other end of the telephone connection. Spoken speech requires the physical movement of the speech articulators: tongue, teeth, and lips. A breath of air must be taken in and released through the constriction of the vocal cords. The expenditure of physical effort during speech probably exceeds that of typing a letter. For many people, it is easier and less effort to type than it is to speak. Perhaps this explains the success of the Internet and e-mail. For example, speaking to a human to obtain a telephone number takes too much effort, and it is much easier to use the Internet to search for telephone numbers.

However, effort also involves a psychological dimension too. The need for a fast reply can affect the choice of communication medium. The letter takes time to be delivered physically and yet more time is needed for a reply. The telephone call and e-mail are instantaneous, and the matter is quickly settled. However, the effort of a telephone call can become large if there is a high probability that the other party will not be there and "telephone tag" will be needed. Also, many people do not respond immediately to an e-mail message. Frustration can thus affect the choice of medium.

Although most people like the concept of video teleconferencing, few people actually use it. This might be because of the effort needed to schedule a teleconference, to prepare material in advance, and to convince the other attendees to teleconference. Perhaps most people seem to think it is easier— less effort—to travel to the distant location for a conventional meeting.

Automatic speech recognition has been suggested for telephone dialing. One would need only to speak the digits of the telephone number to be reached. However, less effort is needed simply to touch the buttons on the telephone dial pad than to speak the same information. Audiotex makes use of a touchtone telephone to retrieve information from a database. The use of automatic speech recognition has been suggested for audiotex applications. I would guess that most people would find that simply entering digits from a keypad is less effort than speaking to the distant database computer.

We see from these examples that a number of factors affect the choice and use of a specific communication medium or modality. The concept of effort, including both physical and other aspects, seems to account for the final choice, but no overall theory has ever been developed.

15

Convergence

Communication media seem to be converging: computers with telecommunication; voice, data, and video with broadband. This section examines the topic of convergence.

COMPUTERS AND TELECOMMUNICATION

One popular past example of convergence was the supposed coming together of computers and telecommunication. The dawn of the information age was claimed to be a result of this convergence of computers and telecommunication. A new term, *compunication*, was even coined decades ago to describe this convergence.

Computers are used to manipulate and process data. They also can be used as a communication device to package, send, receive, and display information. A previous section described and discussed the many uses of computer communication. However, when used for such communication, the computer really is nothing more than an advanced form of teletypewriter. There is nothing new about typing information and then transmitting it as data to a distant location—telegraph machines and teletypewriters have been doing this for well over a century. Large amounts of data are stored in centrally located computer systems, called *database systems*, which can be accessed through telecommunication. In this way, telecommunication can be used to access databases or to perform remote computations. Thus, in this way, computers use telecommunication.

Telecommunication involves the transmission and switching of signals over distance. Computers have internal electronic circuitry that switch and send signals from one component to another, and in this way the functions of the computer are accomplished. The newer electronic and digital switching systems used in telecommunication are controlled by programmable computers. Thus, telecommunication uses computers.

The boundary between computers and telecommunication is distinct, although each uses the other. There most certainly seems to be little convergence in the sense of creating some new communication medium. As far as computers and telecommunication are concerned, convergence appears to be a myth, although the use of telecommunication by computers is quite powerful.

NARROWBAND-BROADBAND CONVERGENCE

The coaxial cable used by the CATV industry is a broadband transmission medium, but the twisted pair of copper wires used to provide local telephone service is a comparatively narrowband medium. Decades ago, it was proposed that CATV's broadband coaxial cable be used to deliver a variety of narrowband two-way services, including voice telephone service and data. This did not happen back then, but seems to be happening today.

A few years ago, telephone companies investigated the use of broadband optical fiber as a replacement for the copper wire presently used to provide local telephone service. It was thought that the telephone company's optical fiber could also be used to deliver a variety of broadband one-way services, including television programming. This too did not happen back then, but is being resurrected today.

The dream of providing voice telephony over the coax of CATV was the rationale behind the purchase of two large CATV companies by AT&T in the late 1990s, only to sell them at a loss a few years later. The dream did not happen. However, the coax of CATV is being used for data access to the Internet over cable modems. The same cable modems are also being used to provide two-way voice telephone service over the Internet. Also, today telephone companies are installing optical fiber to homes in the hope of providing voice, data, and video in competition with CATV companies.

Table 15.1 compares television, telephone service, and Internet access in terms of the directionality and bandwidth of the signal, the type of

Table 15.1. Technological characteristics of different services.

	TELEVISION	TELEPHONE SERVICE	INTERNET/WEB ACCESS
Directionality	one-way	two-way	two-way
Signal Bandwidth	broadband	narrowband	narrow/medium
Network	broadcast	switched	switched
Purpose	entertainment	interpersonal	information
Transmission Medium:			
today	radio waves coaxial cable	copper wire: twisted pair	copper wire: twisted pair coaxial cable
future	optical fiber	optical fiber	optical fiber

network, the purpose of the communication content, and the transmission medium.

In the distant future, all three services will most likely use optical fiber as their transmission medium. However, CATV television is quite different from telephone service and Internet access in all other aspects. The one-way broadcast nature of entertainment television is quite distinct from the two-way switched nature of interpersonal telephone service and Internet access. The convergence of narrowband telephone service with broadband CATV television seems thus far to be a myth. But cable modems are delivering two-way Internet access, and digital subscriber line (DSL) technology is delivering high-speed Internet access over the twisted pairs of copper wires of the telephone companies. The conduit, coaxial cable or twisted-pair, can be used for a variety of services, but this does not mean that the services themselves have converged.

The bandwidth of Internet access is increasing, however. The Internet is increasingly being used to transmit audio and video. These signals, particularly video, require considerable bandwidth, even when compressed digitally.

VIDEO AND TELEPHONY

Today, the copper wire of the telephone company delivers mostly two-way voice telephone service for interpersonal communication, and the coaxial cable of the CATV company delivers mostly one-way television service for entertainment purposes. As stated earlier, optical fiber has the capacity to carry all these services, along with others, to the home over a single transmission medium. This technological ability created much interest in CATV by telephone companies, and the CATV companies have countered

Table 15.2. Categorization of telecommunication-delivered electronic media by content.

CONTENT	DIRECTIONALITY		TRANSMISSION MEDIUM
	two-way switched	one-way broadcast	
voice	telephone		land (wire)
	cellular	AM/FM radio	air (radio)
video		CATV	land (wire)
		VHF/UHF TV	air (radio)
	interpersonal	entertainment	
	PURPOSE		

by expressing interest in providing interpersonal communication services, such as voice telephony.

Table 15.2 categorizes telecommunication-delivered electronic media according to directionality (two-way and one-way) and content (voice and video). The table also presents subcategories for the media according to whether the transmission medium is over land, such as by wire or optical fiber, or over the air, such as by radio.

The conclusion is that today the world of two-way switched voice media is distinct from the world of one-way broadcast video media. Furthermore, the two-way voice media are used mostly for interpersonal purposes while the one-way video media are used mostly for entertainment purposes. There does not appear to be a rationale for convergence of the two worlds, and the convergence of television and telephony would seem to be a myth.

However, new services might appear that overlap the two worlds. For example, the picturephone is a two-way video medium for interpersonal communication. But, the picturephone is decades old and has consistently failed to excite much consumer interest, even after many reincarnations.

TELEVISION-COMPUTER CONVERGENCE

A television receiver uses a cathode ray tube to display the picture. A personal computer likewise uses a cathode ray tube to display text and graphic information. Since both devices use a cathode ray tube for display, computers and television were claimed to be converging. Furthermore, since a computer can be used as a telecommunication device to access remote databases, some form of convergence between television and telecommunication might also occur.

For example, the initial implementation of videotex used the home TV set to display the information accessed over the telephone line from the remote videotex database, as is done with WebTV.

Quite clearly, the television set and the personal computer might both use a CRT or liquid crystal device for display, but otherwise they are distinct. Convergence of the TV set and the personal computer has thus far been a myth.

Television sets of the future will increasingly include sophisticated electronic circuitry to improve and enhance the quality of the received picture, to store portions of the picture, and to control operation of the set. High-definition television will utilize digital encoding and transmission along with additional digital circuitry and processing at the TV set. All this circuitry could be considered a computer, but it would be a special-purpose computer as opposed to the general-purpose computer of the personal computer. However, laptop personal computers are used to play DVDs, and in this way, a form of media convergence has occurred.

VOICE-DATA-VIDEO CONVERGENCE

Voice telephone signals are converted to digital and in this form are transmitted and switched over the telephone network. Data already is a digital signal. Television is increasingly being converted to digital and is being transmitted over various digital transmission media. It appears that the world of telecommunication is going digital. With digital, all signals are converted to a string of binary digits, called *bits*. All bits are simply 0s and 1s, regardless of the signals they represent. The concept of the integration of digitized voice, data, and video on a single digital network is known as an *integrated services digital network*, or *ISDN*, for short.

Thus, in the world of digital, voice telephone signals, data, and video all have the same format. In terms of digital, voice, data, and video are converging. However, in terms of content, purpose, directionality, and other characteristics, the services are distinct. The world of digital is an example of convergence in terms of signal format, but otherwise convergence of voice, data, and video is a myth.

Indeed, in the world of digital, "a bit's a bit." But in the old word of analog, "a hertz's a hertz," and services did not converge but remained separate. The current fascination with all things digital might be a phase that will pass, and sanity will again hopefully prevail.

MEDIA USE

In the late 1980s, the Internet was still a dream and was only starting to evolve from the packet-switched NSFNET. A few years later, the hype about the Internet became a craze and the mantra became "the Internet is everything." Yet the dot-com craze of the Internet collapsed financially in 2001. Is there some way to make sense of the Internet with a reasonable perspective that separates reality from fantasy?

Surveys were made a few years ago of graduate students in New York City and of undergraduate students in Los Angeles to determine their usage of a variety of interpersonal and mass media. The results (shown in table 15.3) are that the graduate students are far heavier users of e-mail than the undergraduates, possibly because many of the graduate students use e-mail at work. The undergraduates download much more music. The undergraduates listen to the radio substantially more, but this is probably because Los Angeles is a great radio town because commuters spend so much time in automobiles.

The media usage from the surveys was converted into bits, and voice traffic was greater then data traffic. It should not be a surprise that voice traffic appears to greatly exceed data traffic. The reason that telephone conversations top the list is that voice telecommunication consumes a vast amount of digital capacity for every second of speech. A single page of text consisting of

Table 15. 3.   Daily media use for students in New York City and Los Angeles.

	DAILY MEDIA USE	
Medium	NYC (graduate students)	Los Angeles (undergraduates)
Telephone	39 mins	36 mins
Cell Phone	19 mins	15 mins
TOTAL VOICE	58 mins	51 mins
E-mails Sent & Received	67	14
Websites	12	7
Software Downloads	0.5	1
A/V Downloads	0.5	4
Broadcast Television	1.5 hrs	2.0 hrs
Videos	0.3 hrs	1.2 hrs
Radio	24 mins	73 mins
Music	75 mins	58 mins
Print Media	148 mins	119 mins

sixty lines of sixty-seven characters each requires about 32,000 bits. This is equivalent to only a half second of digital speech! The average three-minute telephone conversation would generate the same digital information as about 360 pages of text.

Credible data shows tremendous amounts of Internet traffic. Such companies as AT&T have reported more data traffic than voice traffic. But where is all this data traffic coming from? Data for websites shows considerable amounts of traffic at the wee hours of the morning when most humans are sound asleep. Could this background traffic be created by Web crawlers that continuously download and index the entire Web and other forms of computer-to-computer communication?

The trend clearly is toward increased use of the Internet. Data traffic will indeed grow as increasing amounts of software, including updates, are downloaded from the Internet. Various forms of entertainment media, such as MP3 audio, will also be increasingly downloaded over the Internet—again increasing the overall volume of data traffic. Entertainment television and video might be downloaded from the Internet, but the tremendous amounts of capacity required for such an application means that this will not happen until some time in the more distant future. What is happening, though, is the uploading of digital photographs to be shared with family and friends and also to be printed in physical albums.

CROSSINGS

A new medium frequently copies old media for content. Television is a good example of this. Television copied much of radio for its content. CATV, with its ability to carry many more channels than conventional over-the-air VHF/UHF television, copies radio even more; such specialized cable channels as MTV (Music TV) and CNN (Cable News Network) are good examples. Figure 15.1 shows many of the crossings from radio to television.

Not all the content of radio has successfully crossed over to television: classical music stations on FM radio do not yet have a counterpart on television. What is interesting is the success of shopping stations on television, which had no predecessor on radio. This could be a case where radio could learn from television, and perhaps some shopping stations on AM radio will appear.

RADIO		TELEVISION
pop/rock	> >	MTV
news	> >	CNN
drama	> >	soap operas
variety shows	> >	variety shows
movies	> >	movies
talk shows	> >	guest shows
	> >	shopping network
classical music	> >	opera and music

FIGURE 15.1
Crossings from radio to television

TEXT AND RADIO

Teletext is a textual adjunct to broadcast television. An interesting question is whether there are opportunities for textual adjuncts to other broadcast media, such as radio, for example.

A teletext-like service for FM radio would make much sense. One would broadcast text over the air along with the FM signal. One valuable application would be while listening to music. The text could identify the composer, the work, and the performer. The text could be displayed on a one-line LCD panel, perhaps the same LCD panel that displays the station number. In this way, the listener would have information about what was being listened to without having to wait for the announcer to make an announcement, perhaps slurring and mispronouncing the words.

The Internet has become an adjunct to radio broadcasting. Radio programs are also broadcast over the Internet. But the Internet is used as a way to obtain more information on a program that has been broadcast, for example, obtaining more information about a work heard on a classical music station.

REFERENCES

Bohlin, Erik, Karolina Brodin, Anders Lundgren, and Bertil Thorngren, eds. *Convergence in Communications and Beyond.* Amsterdam: Elsevier, 2000.

Collis, David J., P. William Bane, and Stephen P. Bradley. "Winners and Losers." In *Competing in the Age of Digital Convergence*, edited by David B. Yoffie. Boston: Harvard Business School Press, 1997, 159–200.

16

Industry Structure

The communication industry can be broadly organized into two major segments: (1) the provision and sale of services and (2) the manufacturing and sale of products. Adopting terminology from the computer industry, the provision of service is called *software*, and the provision of products is called *hardware*. An example from the world of television will make this distinction clearer. Television receivers are products, but the production and broadcasting of television programs is a service. Television receivers are manufactured and sold by companies and through outlets quite separate from the companies that produce and broadcast television programs. Most mass media have both service and product aspects.

The service and product segments of the communication industry are described in this chapter. We start with mass media.

MASS MEDIA SERVICE PROVIDERS

Entertainment radio and television are provided by broadcasters. The radio broadcast industry consists mostly of a number of small, independent stations, although some of them are affiliated with radio networks and rely on the network for much of their program material. The television broadcast industry in the United States was dominated in the past by three major networks: CBS, NBC, and ABC. Local television broadcasting was performed by local stations that were affiliated with the networks and obtained much of their program material from the networks. Cable television (CATV) operators obtain their program material from a wide variety of sources, including material broadcast over the air by the networks and the local affiliates. CATV operators also obtain program material from providers that operate networks using communication satellite distribution only to CATV operators. Ted Turner's Cable News Network (CNN) is one such example. The wide variety of program material available over CATV has been a major factor in the reduction of viewers for the three major broadcast networks.

Television broadcasters package and distribute video material produced by others, in addition to news and other content they produce themselves. This is somewhat similar to the motion picture industry, in which movies are made by the major studios and are then distributed to motion picture theaters and chains. Movies ultimately become videos, which are sold for VCR and DVD viewing at home and are then rented to viewers by local video stores. Along the way, many motion pictures make their way into airplanes for viewing there too. A whole science, as described by David Waterman, has arisen to maximize profits through the appropriate timing of these different releases and distributions of the same motion picture.

Rock videos broadcast over specialized CATV networks have created a whole new industry. Rock video networks essentially copy rock radio stations in format, but have added a video dimension to audio. Perhaps a similar possibility exists for opera, but perhaps not, since much classical music listening is an audio-only experience. Audio recordings are made by the various record companies and are sold through record stores. Recordings are provided to AM and FM radio stations for broadcast over the air.

Print media are provided by the publishers of books, newspapers, and magazines. Communication satellites have made possible truly national newspapers, such as the *Wall Street Journal* and *USA Today*, which are printed and distributed locally. Books rely upon local stores and book clubs for distribution. Magazines too are distributed through local newsstands, but also rely on subscription sales. Newspapers are delivered locally by local delivery people and are also sold by newsstands. The newsstand of the past with its friendly owner has been replaced by impersonal vending machines in many cities.

MASS MEDIA SYSTEM

Many mass media are supported by the sale of advertising. The relationship between advertisers, distributors, content creators, and packagers creates a vast, interrelated system. Figure 16.1 attempts to show these interrelationships.

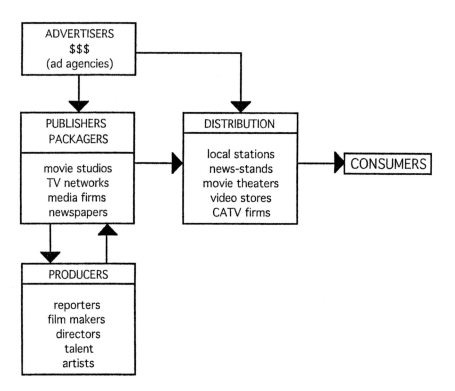

FIGURE 16.1
The interrelated mass media system

There is a mutual dependency of all participants in the media system: everyone needs everyone else. Ultimately, the consumer purchases advertised products and in this way pays for the costs of production and distribution.

MASS MEDIA EQUIPMENT PROVIDERS

Television receivers are manufactured by consumer electronics firms and are sold in various retail stores. Compact disc players, videocassette recorders, DVD players, MP3 players, and stereophonic sound systems and components are some of the other items manufactured by the consumer electronics industry.

Digital computers are increasingly being used as media hubs to store and process digital media, such as digital photographs and digital music. The flat-panel displays used for laptop computers have grown in size and are sold for television display. What this means is the distinction between consumer electronics and digital computers is continuing to become blurred, although the purpose for their use remains distinct.

INTERPERSONAL COMMUNICATION INDUSTRY

Telecommunication service is provided by local and long-distance common carriers, so called since they carry all traffic and do not change its contents in any way. Local telephone service is provided by local exchange carriers, mostly the Bell companies in the United States. Long-distance service is provided by interexchange carriers, such as AT&T, MCI, and Sprint. The telecommunication network carries not only voice telephone calls but facsimile calls also.

Specialized data networks, such as the Internet, are operated by specialized common carriers. Access to the Internet is supplied by Internet access providers. Digital voice can be converted into packets and carried over the Internet, a service known as *voice over the Internet protocol (VoIP)*. Thus, data carriers offer competition to conventional voice common carriers.

Physical delivery of the mail is performed by the U.S. Postal Service. Overnight air delivery of small parcels is performed by a number of air-express companies, and even the U.S. Postal Service initiated its own Express Mail in response to the competition from these air-express carriers. Most small packages are delivered by the United Parcel Service (UPS), and UPS too initiated one-day and two-day air service in response to competition.

Computers are manufactured by computer companies and are sold in computer stores and specialty electronics stores and by mail order. Computer programs are written by individuals and are marketed by various software distributors. Software is sold in computer stores and bookstores and by mail order.

Telephones, facsimile units, answer-and-record machines, and cellular telephones are manufactured by telephone-equipment companies and are sold to consumers in a variety of retail outlets. Telephone switching and transmission systems are manufactured by various electronics companies and are sold directly to the common carriers.

Some other equipment and products provided as part of the communication media industry are cameras, film, copiers, and typewriters. Copiers, typewriters, and computers used as word processors are all part of a growing office-supply business aimed at the consumer and small businesses. This office-supply business includes paper.

Newspapers and other print publishers need vast amounts of paper and printing and binding services. These products and services are purchased by service suppliers and not directly by consumers.

FINANCIAL ASPECTS

As was stated earlier, most communication consists of two components. One component is the provision of hardware, such as a telephone instrument or a television receiver. The other component is the provision of content or software, such as the provision of telephone service or the television programming. It is interesting to examine the revenue generated by each component in the United States using data from the *Statistical Abstract of the United States: 2004–2005.*

In 2002, the total revenue from the provision of telecommunication services (such as telephone and cellular service) was $353 billion. However, the sale of telephones and associated equipment generated only $2.6 billion.

Radio broadcasting generated $15 billion in revenues, but the sale of radios generated only about $0.8 billion. Clearly, the production of content, or software, is the major component of the radio industry. The sale of television receivers, VCRs, camcorders, and other video equipment for the home generated revenues of $19 billion in 2002. Television broadcasting, including CATV service, generated revenues of $81 billion, but the sale of video products for the home generated considerably less, as stated above.

In 2002, the total revenue for personal computer hardware was $31 billion, while the sale of software for personal computers generated a total revenue of $20 billion.

The preceding revenues, along with the percentage of revenue generated by software compared to total revenue, are summarized in table 16.1. The conclusion from this analysis is that the sale of software, meaning content and service, generally far exceeds the revenue from the sale of equipment. The exception is the personal computer industry, for which the sale of computer hardware exceeds the sale of software and computer services. But the bottom-line profitability of the sale of computer software is probably considerably more than the sale of hardware.

Table 16.1. Communication segment revenues for 2002.

	REVENUES		
SEGMENT	HARDWARE	SOFTWARE & SERVICE	PERCENT (software/total)
telecommunication	$2.6 B	$353 B	99%
radio	$0.8 B est.	$15 B	95%
television	$19 B	$81 B	81%
personal computer	$31 B	$20 B	40%

If I think about my own personal expenditures, this conclusion is not surprising. My monthly telephone bill for local, long-distance, and wireless service is well over $100, but my $30 telephone instrument lasts for years. A CD player sells for about $30, but my yearly purchase of CDs used to be many times that amount. My computer is mostly used for word processing, using software that cost about $100. However, the computer itself cost about $1,200, and a laser printer, about $200.

Thus, in general, software is the business to be in for the entertainment and telecommunication industries. Manufacturing and the sale of products do not generate much revenue compared to the provision of service and content. The exception is the personal computer, for which the sale of hardware produces more revenue than software, but the profit margins are much higher for software. Also, many people probably spend more for books about their computer than for computer software.

REFERENCE

Waterman, David. "Prerecorded Home Video and the Distribution of Theatrical Feature Films." In *Video Media Competition*, edited by Eli M. Noam. New York: Columbia University Press, 1985, 221–243.

IV

THINKING STRATEGICALLY

The preceding material of this book developed a framework for understanding media. But now we need a methodology for using this knowledge in a strategic manner to perform critical analyses. Part IV of this book presents a methodology for doing that.

In the foreword to *Highway of Dreams*, Abe Zarem compared the hype of the information superhighway to the tulip fever in Holland nearly four hundred years ago and predicted the coming of a "tulip time in telecommunications" (Zarem 1997, iii–vi). Zarem clearly foresaw the coming financial collapse of the dot-com bubble as overpromoted Internet stocks reached a peak and then collapsed. He wisely stated that "our principal need is for strategic thinking." Yet, even after the bubble burst, the Internet and the World Wide Web are an entrenched and essential form of communication and commerce.

But a new wave of overpromotion and hype is again beginning to swell. How do we separate the real from the unreal? How can we perform strategic and critical analyses of communication products, services, and ventures—as called for by Zarem?

The methodology for strategic analysis is based on the premise that five dimensions—or factors—shape the future. These five factors are technology, finance and economics, policy and government, business and management, and consumers and their behavior. Any new communication venture must be examined critically in terms of each of these five factors. The factors are links in a chain, and the overall probability of success will be determined primarily by the weakest link. The basic considerations of each factor are described, and examples are given of the application of the methodology to specific communication products and services.

17

Five Factors for Shaping the Future

The future of the communication industry faces considerable uncertainty, perhaps, some people believe, because of extremely rapid advances in technology. Segments of the communication industry appear to be converging, and boundaries are blurring between what were clearly defined segments of yesteryear. Managing and choosing wisely is quite challenging in such times of fundamental transformation.

The past years have been a roller-coaster ride, as the hype of such terms as *multimedia, convergence, synergy, interactive, the Internet, cyber,* and *digital* became overwhelming, and the bubble burst with the dot-com collapse on Wall Street. We were told to accelerate onto the information superhighway or risk being left behind in a cloud of semiconductor dust.

The media mania of the information superhighway ultimately ran out of steam, yet digital and cyber technology is here to stay as a major part of our lives. Clearly, with hindsight, we recognize that overenthusiasm, overpromotion, and overfascination with technology for its own sake is not the way to understand the future. The books and writings of the mid-1990s certainly fueled the euphoria (Gates 1995; Negroponte 1995). Huge mergers of media and telecommunication firms occurred, but nearly all became nightmares for those involved, except for the authors of books attempting to explain the collapse (Goldstein 2005). But is there any real way to illuminate the end of these tunnels?

This part of the book presents a relatively simple and straightforward methodology for understanding and illuminating the future. The methodology is for performing a strategic and critical analysis of a new opportunity for any business, product, or service. The methodology is based on a careful consideration of each of the five factors that shape the future and thus determine the prospects for success or failure of any new opportunity. In addition, consideration should be given to a historical perspective, since indeed "the past is prologue to the future." Many "new" ideas are simply old ideas in disguise.

After listing the five factors, a short overview of each factor is given. In a following chapter, examples are described of the use of these factors to analyze various communication products and services.

FIVE FACTORS

The success or failure of any new product or service or business venture is determined by a large number of factors or considerations, any one of which might be the most critical. All these considerations seem to cluster in the following five areas:

(1) technology,
(2) finance and economics,
(3) policy and regulation,
(4) management and business, and
(5) consumers and their needs.

Each factor will be discussed in more detail in this chapter. There is no need to delve deeply into each factor, since it is usually quite obvious which ones will most strongly affect the overall success.

The overall probability of success depends on each factor, and like links in a chain, as depicted in figure 17.1, the overall success depends mostly on the weakest link.

FIRST FACTOR: TECHNOLOGY

Many new products and services come from advances in technology and technological innovations. Although most advances in technology are evolutionary rather than revolutionary, the term *revolution* is used by the media to characterize nearly everything—leading to much hype. Technology is mysterious to most people, who seem to lack the fundamental knowledge to grasp the basic principles of communication technology, which is why there is a technology tutorial as an appendix to this book.

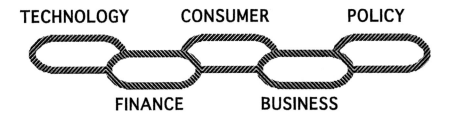

FIGURE 17.1
The five factors are like the links in a chain: the overall success is only as probable as the weakest link.

Advances in digital computer technology are resulting in smaller devices with larger capacities in storage and processing power, and at the same time, everything is becoming less costly. It seems that the pace of advances in technology is accelerating.

Communication products and services must be easy to use for consumers, and thus the human interface is an essential portion of any overall design. A prime example of this is the user-friendly pull-down menu of the windows-based computer interface, innovated at the Xerox Palo Alto Research Center and incorporated initially by Apple Computer into its Macintosh computer.

All media seem to be digital, but consumers are analog. Thus all digital signals must ultimately be converted to an analog form to be used by humans. The digital format offers immunity against noise and distortion, but there are analog-based methods that can accomplish immunity too. An overfascination with digital could result in missed opportunities for analog innovations.

Technology needs to be taken from the laboratory to manufacturing in actual products, and this process takes time. An idea for an improvement in a product should not be compared with products in the market, since one does not know what advances others are planning in their laboratories, and the time required to market introduction can be long.

SECOND FACTOR: FINANCE AND ECONOMICS
Any new business, product, or service must ultimately generate a financial profit and a positive return on the initial investment. Hence, finance and economics are an important factor in determining success. Many books

have been written and advanced degrees given in finance and in economics, but a few basic principles enable simple "back of the envelope" analyses.

An examination of where the revenues have been in the communication industry is enlightening. Box 17.1 gives the revenues in 2002 for different major segments of the communication industry. Telecommunication services clearly was the largest, easily dwarfing cinema and television. Physical delivery services by the three largest shippers was larger than the entire computer software business.

Any new product, service, or business requires an initial investment for its development. The investors making this investment want to receive their principal back along with an adequate profit, or rate of return, on the investment. Usually, the investors do not want to wait forever for this return and expect to receive it within a reasonable period of time—a few years, not decades. The payment to the investor consists of the return of principal plus interest on the initial investment.

As an example, assume a CATV company is acquired at a price that amounts to $3,000 per CATV subscriber. Assume the purchaser wants to obtain a return of 10 percent and recoup the original investment within ten years. Although an equation should be used to perform the calculation accurately, a very simple approximation is $300 per year in interest and an additional $300 per year to recoup the principal. Thus, the total yearly return must be about $600 per CATV subscriber. If the average CATV bill is $30 per month, the required return is impossible, and the price of $3,000 per CATV subscriber is excessive.

The annual report of a business documents its profitability, comparing financial performance over a number of years. The total revenue is listed and then

BOX 17.1

$353B   Telecommunication services

$195B   Cinema and television services

$143B   Publishing (newspapers, books, magazines, directories)

$118B   Physical delivery (USPS + UPS + FedEx)

$89B   Computer software

various deductions are subtracted for such items as the direct operating expense of doing business; the cost of selling, general, and administrative (SG&A) matters; and depreciation and amortization. This gives the operating income, from which interest and taxes are then deducted to obtain the net income. Payment of dividends to the shareholders is made from the net income, which hopefully is positive and not a loss. Some businesses operate at a loss quite regularly, and a measure known as EBITDA (earnings before interest, taxes, depreciation, and amortization) is used to measure their financial performance.

Because of hype and great expectations, the stock of a company might become greatly overvalued. When this happens, the company might attempt to convert its overvalued paper wealth into real wealth by acquiring another company, using the value of its stock to complete the purchase. Such bubbles usually burst.

THIRD FACTOR: POLICY AND REGULATION

Much of telecommunication and communication is regulated by the government at both the federal and the state level. The *Communications Act of 1934* created the Federal Communications Commission (FCC) to regulate telecommunication in the United States. The FCC continues to regulate telecommunication, even though competition is to be preferred to orders by government bureaucrats.

The *Telecommunications Act of 1996* was an attempt to reduce regulation and to promote competition in telecommunication. The Internet was both promoted and protected by the provisions of the act. Digital broadcast television was promoted, with analog transmission to cease in about ten years. Internet indecency was prohibited, but these provisions were overturned by the United States Supreme Court.

Government will always want to exert its influence in shaping the future, justifying such meddling as being in the public interest or somehow protecting the public. But government is subject to political pressures and also the lobbying influence of industry and various groups. And government policy can change dramatically.

A problem occurs when government advocates a specific technology. Government rarely has the knowledge to evaluate technological options fairly and hence must rely instead on political factors—a sure path to big errors in judgment.

FOURTH FACTOR: BUSINESS/MANAGEMENT

Products and services must be delivered to consumers, and this requires the formal structure of a business. The structure of these businesses includes the management of the firm and how the business is operated.

Clearly, as its first priority, a business should be responsive to its customers—the only real reason a business exists is to serve its customers. But customers are frequently ignored—or are viewed as a chore—by many businesses that seem to have forgotten "the customer is always right."

Mergers have become quite popular in business. But most mergers are outright acquisitions of one company by another. The term *merger* is frequently used to create the appearance of a friendly marriage when in fact the merger is the total consumption of one firm by another. History shows that most mergers fail to achieve their objectives, and many are outright failures. But mergers can make good sense, particularly when the merger achieves industry consolidation by combining two competitors.

A business is managed by people, and interpersonal factors usually determine most business decisions—not complex business cases. Most mergers occur because of personal factors involving the personalities of top management. Understand the personalities, and the rationale—or lack of rationale—of mergers will become clearer.

FIFTH FACTOR: CONSUMER/MARKET

Ultimately, people—consumers, managers, government officials—seem to be the most important factor in shaping the future. The human dimension has always been essential, but it is all too frequently ignored. Leadership is an important aspect of the human dimension, but it too is frequently clouded by hype and euphoria.

Market trends are very important in understanding the future. For example, most people in the United States now obtain their television from either cable (CATV) or satellite (DBS). This means that over-the-air broadcast TV is dying.

The purchase of a product or service by consumers usually means a transfer from some other expenditure. The average monthly expenditures per household in the United States, tabulated in box 17.2, show that food comes first over expenditures for media.

BOX 17.2

$827	Household food
$189	Utilities (electricity, gas, water, oil)
$170	Gasoline
$97	Telephone service
$57	Audio and video hardware
$50	Cable/satellite service
$38	Computer (hardware and software)
$30	Books and maps
$29	Magazines and newspapers
$18	DVD/videocassette rentals and purchases
$18	Internet access
$7	Admission to movie theaters

Note: Numbers are for 2004.
Sources: Courtesy of Dr. John Carey from the U.S. Dept. of Commerce, J. D. Power, *Video Business*, and the *Wall Street Journal*. ∎

The determination of consumer needs and behaviors is a challenging task. Market research claims to accomplish such a determination. Yet how a question is posed will frequently cloud the response. Such techniques as focus groups are highly subjective and are not statistically significant, but sometimes are overused to justify market entry. Firms with their own internal market research units should keep them separate and protect them to maintain objectivity.

REFERENCES

Gates, Bill. *The Road Ahead*. New York: Vintage Books, 1995.

Goldstein, Fred R. *The Great Telecom Meltdown*. Norwood, Mass.: Artech House, 2005.

Negroponte, Nicholas. *Being Digital*. New York: Vintage Books, 1995.

18

Historical Perspectives

Many things that seem new and novel frequently are simply old products and services that have been reinvented and promoted anew, sometimes with a new twist or repackaging. Thus, an important question to be answered from a historical perspective is whether the product or service is really new. The perspective obtained from historical information can frequently dispel much hype and offer a more sober analysis.

We are frequently told to have faith—that bold new ideas can be destroyed from too much initial criticism and overanalysis. Faith might be appropriate for religion, but faith is not appropriate for making business decisions. Indeed, "the past is prologue to the future,"not blind faith coupled with much hope (Robichaux 1993). History does seem to repeat, and we seem doomed to repeat our past mistakes. One way out of this dilemma is to study history and learn from it.

IS IT NEW?

A reason for studying the past is to determine whether the service or product is truly new. Much of what is promoted as innovative or as novel is frequently a resurrection of the past. This is not to say that past mistakes are always doomed to failure—market conditions, technology, and policy can change to turn a past failure into a success.

In the early 1990s, much publicity was generated by the media and by the advocates of an "information superhighway." But the concept of such an information highway was already decades old, and the term was as nebulous in the

1990s as it was decades ago when the terms *wired city* and *electronic highway* were first coined. The information superhighway was just more hype, as one reporter had the courage to state in a piece titled "Highway of Hype."

Telecommunication is frequently promoted as the solution to a host of social ills—for education and medicine, in particular. But tele-education and telemedicine are decades old, and most uses for telecommunication in medicine and education are mostly applications of the familiar telephone, perhaps enhanced with video.

Although the packet-switching technology of the Internet is decades old, the simplicity of the World Wide Web is relatively new. But the concept of electronic access to information in the home was tried in the 1980s with a system known as videotex. It used the home TV set to display information accessed from a centralized database. Videotex was a failure. The World Wide Web is a success, probably because it allows access to many decentralized databases in a user-friendly fashion.

MERGERS

It is challenging to name one corporate merger that has been successful in the communication industry. There are so many failed mergers that any sensible investor would flee from any proposed merger, and it seems that only the banks and consultants that put together the mergers benefit financially. Many of the failed mergers were promised to achieve synergy in the cyber world of multimedia and corporate efficiency.

The list of failed mergers includes AOL's acquisition of TimeWarner, Disney's acquisition of ABC, and AT&T's acquisition of NCR (only to divest NCR after a few years). The first two were justified in the name of the synergies that would occur, but these synergies were elusive and never materialized. In fact, they probably never had any prospects, other than media value in selling the acquisitions to the Wall Street investor community. The AT&T acquisition of NCR was made because AT&T had become convinced that its future was in computers, and it had failed with its attempt to create its own computer business internally. In the end, the foray into computers by AT&T was a nightmare and a big mistake—all of which was clearly predictable. The acquisition of the Compaq computer business by Hewlett-Packard in 2002 resulted in decreased profits for Hewlett-Packard, along with a confused sense of purpose and mission (*Economist* August 21, 2004).

FIBER TO THE HOME: YET AGAIN!

In 2004, Verizon announced its plans to install optical fiber directly to three million homes by the end of 2005 at a cost of $2.5 billion (Rhoads 2004). The optical fiber offers a host of services, such as conventional telephone service, fast Internet access, and high-definition television, and will offer a host of novel services yet to be invented. But this futuristic high-technology vision is not new.

In the late 1960s, a "broadband communication network" was first proposed. In 1971, when the terms *wired city, electronic highway,* and *two-way cable* first appeared, they all promised a broadband highway of many services to the home. In the late 1970s, a number of trials of two-way broadband access were conducted, such as HI-OVIS in Japan, Warner's Qube in Columbus, Ohio, and two-way cable in Irvine, California. In the mid-1990s, Bell Atlantic (now Verizon) connected over five thousand homes in Dover Township, New Jersey, to an optical fiber system offering a variety of services, including conventional telephone service and video programming (Noll 1997). The Dover Township system mysteriously was terminated and then vanished in corporate amnesia.

THE DIGITAL MYSTIQUE

Today, there is an overfascination with all things digital. Yet digital is decades old, going back to 1948 when Bell Labs scientists first proposed it in the form of pulse code modulation to multiplex telephone signals. Digital art, digital animation, digital speech, and digital music were all invented at Bell Labs in the 1960s. Indeed, today's digital audio, digital video, and digital computers are quite impressive, but the concepts are not novel.

Humans are analog—not digital. Thus digital signals must always be converted into some form of analog signal in order to be seen or heard by humans. There will always be a place for analog, even in today's world of digital. The content—not the technology—will always be the most important. Digital offers advantages in terms of quality reproduction by overcoming the problems of noise and distortion. But most consumers couldn't care less whether what they listen to or watch is analog or digital. Program content matters most. But yet the word *digital* continues to overfascinate those who should study history a little to gain more composure and dispel hype.

PICTUREPHONE

Nearly every science fiction movie shows some form of two-way picture-phone. Yet, all attempts to market a picturephone have consistently failed (Noll 1992).

An early picturephone was demonstrated by AT&T at the New York World's Fair in 1964. About seven hundred people who used the demonstration picturephone were asked their opinions, and although about one-half of those interviewed did not believe it was important to see the other person during a telephone call, AT&T interpreted the results positively and went ahead with a massive development project and introduced the service in a few cities in the early 1970s. The service was a dismal failure. The results of market research, performed to understand the failure, indicated there was little need for face-to-face communication. Thus the consumer factor was the major reason for the lack of success—technologically, the original picturephone was a marvel.

In 1992, somehow suffering from corporate amnesia regarding its past experience with the picturephone, AT&T introduced a color visual telephone that worked over regular phone lines. It too was a market failure, as were video telephones introduced by Mitsubishi and others a few years later.

Yet, interest in video telephones continues. Today, some wireless cell phones include a camera, thereby making the cell phone also a picturephone in the sense that it can be used to take a digital photograph, possibly of a scene or of the user's face. But it is both awkward and silly to be speaking to someone and at the same time holding the cell phone away and aiming it at your face. But some people do want to show the person they are speaking to where they are in order to share the experience.

MARKET GROWTH

The number of years that it took in the United States for companies to achieve significant market penetration for such communication services as the telephone, the phonograph, and CATV is sobering, as shown in table 18.1. However, other services, such as radio and monochrome TV, achieved market penetrations of 50 percent in only ten years. Most recently, the Internet achieved a 50 percent penetration in about ten years.

Although some communication services and products were slow, but steady, in terms of achieving significant market penetration, other services

TABLE 18.1. Market penetrations.

SERVICE	YEARS	MARKET PENETRATION
telephone	70	50%
phonograph	55	50%
CATV	45	62%
radio	10	50%
monochrome TV	10	50%

have been real losers and never achieved any significant market penetration. One good example of a consistent loser has been the picturephone, mentioned previously. The eight-track tape was yet another loser.

REFERENCES

"Losing the HP Way." *Economist* 372, no. 8389 (August 21, 2004): 49–50.

Noll, A. Michael. "Anatomy of a Failure: Picturephone Revisited." *Telecommunication Policy* 16, no. 4 (May/June 1992): 307–316.

———. *Highway of Dreams: A Critical View along the Information Superhighway.* Mahwah, N.J.: Lawrence Erlbaum, 1997.

Rhoads, Christopher. "Bringing Fiber Home." *Wall Street Journal*, August 19, 2004, B1–B2.

Robichaux, Mark. "Highway of Hype." *Wall Street Journal*, November 29, 1993, A7.

Using the Five Factors

Any analytic technique is only valuable if it is easy to use and if it gives accurate results. In this section, examples are presented of the application of the five factors to analyze various communication services and products.

WHAT IS IT?

The very first step in any analysis is to define precisely the product or service to be analyzed. Many products and services are so nebulously defined as to be almost anything or even to have changing definitions. Some products and services attempt to be so many different things that they are really nothing but a source of confusion for most consumers. Any new product or service is only as real as its definition. Once the product or service has been clearly defined, the five factors can be applied.

OVERALL PROBABILITY OF SUCCESS

Each of the five factors has its own probability of success (p_i), which can be estimated either by a good guess or by asking a panel of experts. The overall probability (P) can then be estimated as the product of the five probabilities, or

$$P = \prod_1^5 p_i$$

This equation clearly is an estimate, since the factors are not completely independent of each other.

One reason for assigning a probability of success to each factor is to identify those factors with the lowest probabilities. These are the factors that will most strongly affect the final outcome and will thus require the most attention if the product or service is ever to succeed.

LOW EARTH ORBIT (LEO) WIRELESS SERVICE

Cellular service covers the planet, offering instant telephonic communication at a fair price to consumers, and has been available for decades now in most countries. Yet, in the 1990s, wireless communication was proposed using communication satellites placed at various orbits about the earth. Geostationary orbits (GEOs) of the earth are at such a great height that serious delay in communication is encountered. Hence, low earth orbits (LEOs) were proposed. The Motorola Iridium system proposed to utilize seventy-seven satellites in six polar orbits about five hundred miles above the surface of the earth and was actually placed in service using sixty-six satellites toward the end of the 1990s at a cost of nearly $4 billion. It was a commercial failure. The strategic analysis technique described in this book explains this failure.

Technology

The technological challenges of LEOs are many, and although solutions are available, the technology is very complex and costly. The LEO unit on Earth requires a fair amount of power to transmit to the LEO satellite. Complex switching and coordination between satellites is required since the satellites pass rapidly overhead during a call.

Finance

Most of the earth's surface is water, and thus most of the time the satellites will be over oceans and not of any use. This means that the useful time of the costly satellites is low. Thus, the costly investment needed to launch the entire constellation of satellites will be very difficult to recover over a reasonable period.

Policy

Many countries regulate telecommunication. Thus, licenses will be needed to offer LEO wireless service. If the firm offering the service were based in the United States, some countries might invoke nationalism to keep the United States out of their markets.

Business

Motorola has been manufacturing wireless phones and equipment and thus understands the wireless market. However, a business operation to sell the service would be required.

Consumer/Market

Wireless cellular service is already available and is firmly entrenched. LEO wireless service offered nothing new compared to cellular wireless, other than the ability to make a wireless call in the middle of an ocean or in those remote places not served by cellular service—and these are not large markets. Here thus is very little—or even no—need for LEO wireless, unless it were considerably cheaper than cellular wireless, which it was not.

Probabilities of success for each factor can be estimated as (1) technology: 0.5, (2) finance: 0.3, (3) policy: 0.3, (4) business: 0.8, and (5) consumer/market: 0.1. Multiplying these five probabilities gives an overall probability of success of only 0.004—a definite failure.

Iridium declared bankruptcy in 1999, was acquired by investors, and then was contracted by the U.S. government to provide wireless military and emergency services. Other extraterrestrial low and middle earth orbit systems, such as Globastar and Teledesic, suspended their plans after the Iridium bankruptcy.

WEBTV

WebTV offered access to the Internet using an adapter that connected to the telephone line and used the home TV set for display of the information. Technologically, WebTV was easy for the consumer to use and to install. However, at $300 for the adapter and $25 per month for access, it was costly—although it did avoid the need for a personal computer. However, the home TV did not have enough resolution to display more than a dozen lines of text and was usually situated in the living room. But the real problem was that those consumers who would be the initial adopters already had personal computers and Internet access. The five-factor analysis predicted a flop—which is what actually occurred.

INTERNET PHONE AND VOIP

The basic idea of using the Internet for telephone calls is quite old. In its initial form, Internet telephony required the use of a personal computer along

TABLE 19.1. Examples of strategic and critical analyses.

TOPIC	TECHNOLOGY	FINANCE	CONSUMER	BUSINESS	POLICY	OVERALL
Videophone	OK [0.9]	OK [0.8]	NO [0.05]	OK [1.0]	OK [1.0]	FAILURE [0.04]
Audio CD	OK [1.0]	OK [1.0]	OK [1.0] • Sounds Great • Easy to Use	OK [1.0]	OK [1.0]	SUCCESS [1.0]
Web TV	OK [0.9]	Unclear [0.4] Costly	NO [0.1] • Web Literacy • Early Adopters	OK [1.0]	OK [1.0]	FAILURE [0.04]
Internet Phone	Problems [0.5]	OK but False [0.2]	OK [0.5] • Need PC • Extra Call	OK [1.0]	Issues Exist [0.2]	FAILURE [0.01]
Low Earth Orbit Wireless Telephony	Uncertain [0.5]	Costly [0.3]	UNCLEAR [0.1] • Cellular Exists	OK [0.8]	Issues Exist [0.3]	FAILURE [0.004]
Powerline Communication	Uncertain [0.2]	Costly [0.2]	OK [1.0]	Issues Exist [0.4]	Issues Exist [0.5]	FAILURE [0.008]

with specialized software and could only be used to call another personal computer with the identical software. Internet telephony was "free," or only as costly as an Internet connection to an access provider. The Internet phone call avoided the costly access charges paid by long-distance companies to the local telephone companies and thus had a false economics created by government-mandated access charges. The analysis correctly concluded that such Internet phones would be a failure.

Voice over the Internet protocol (VoIP) offered some new twists on this old idea of using the Internet for voice telephone service. Rather than use the personal computer, dedicated electronics are used in a box, which the consumer could connect to a cable modem or DSL modem and between the existing phones in the home. The awkwardness of the personal computer is thus avoided. The call is completed at the distant end using the facilities of the VoIP service provider, and thus the called party does not require any special equipment or software. The pricing of the service avoids access charges. VoIP seems to be a success.

POWERLINE COMMUNICATION (PLC)

The power line carries electric power to the home in the form of alternating current at a frequency of 60 Hz and a nominal voltage of 110 volts. Powerline communication (PLC) proposes the use of the copper wires that carry electric power to also carry communication signals. There are many challenges to be solved with PLC.

Technology

There are many electric transformers along the power line, which step down the voltage as the line gets closer to the home. These transformers are designed for 60 Hz and not for the higher frequencies needed for communication. They must therefore be bypassed, which is challenging technologically and a costly complication. Power lines are not shielded and thus pick up much electric noise, and they also radiate higher frequencies, such as would be used with PLC. It would be very challenging to solve all these technological problems at a reasonable cost. Thus the technology factor has a low probability of success.

Policy and Finance

Electric utility companies are highly regulated. Any cross-subsidization of an unregulated PLC operation by the regulated utility operation would most likely not be allowed. Delays in obtaining regulatory permission to supply PLC would likely be encountered also.

Business

Electric utility companies know nothing of the two-way communication business. Also, both CATV operators and telephone companies already provide high-speed Internet access at reasonable prices. PLC would be a very late arrival, if the technological and other challenges were solved.

Consumer

Consumers clearly have a need for high-speed Internet access. The technological challenges, coupled with the regulatory issues and the late arrival of PLC, if it were to work technically, result in an extremely low overall probability of success for PLC.

LESSONS FOR THE FUTURE

There are lessons to be learned from history and from a more critical perspective. We need to understand past failures and not repeat the mistakes that caused them. Clearly, innovation is not repeating the mistakes of the past. Technology clearly is an important factor in shaping the future—but technology-push should be avoided. Other factors are as important—if not even more so. Much progress is incremental and slow—true revolutions are quite rare.

Although much is written about discovering the so-called killer application that will assure success, the real challenge is to avoid getting killed while looking for it! Although faith is fine for religion, it has no place in business and in making business decisions.

Much has been written about convergence, but convergence seems to be a myth. However, boundaries are blurring between media and between communication sectors, which can indeed create new opportunities. Consumers want to be entertained, and indeed "content is king." Much interpersonal communication is narrowband, but most entertainment is broadband.

Appendix

Technology Tutorial

SIGNALS

The concept of a signal is fundamental to communication. A signal, by changing with time, is able to convey information. The position of flags in the semaphore were the signals that conveyed information. Modern communication systems create and utilize signals to transmit information. The signals in modern communication systems are frequently electrical, since in this form they can be easily amplified, modified, and transmitted.

Any signal can be plotted as a function of time to show its shape and variation. The shape of a signal is called a *waveform* or *waveshape*, as depicted in figure A.1. Time is plotted along the x-axis, or abscissa. The height, or amplitude, of the waveform at each instant in time is plotted along the y-axis, or ordinate. Signals have maximum amplitudes in the positive and in the negative directions. Many waveforms are symmetric, having the same shape in both directions, or polarities. Engineers utilize a device called an *oscilloscope* to display the shape of signals.

Some waveforms have a basic shape that keeps repeating itself in time. Such waveforms are called *periodic*. Many periodic waveforms are named according to their basic shape, such as the square wave and the sawtooth wave. Other waveforms have random shapes with no obvious pattern, such as noise. The waveform for speech looks periodic during voiced sounds, such as "ah," and looks like noise during fricatives, such as "sh."

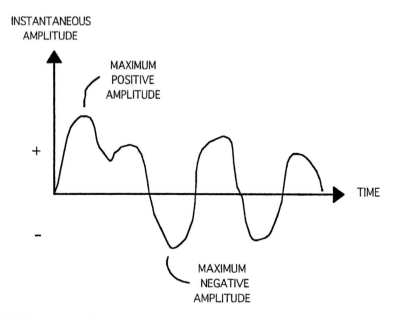

INSTANTANEOUS
AMPLITUDE

MAXIMUM
POSITIVE
AMPLITUDE

+

TIME

—

MAXIMUM
NEGATIVE
AMPLITUDE

FIGURE A.1

A signal has a particular shape—called its *waveform* or *waveshape*—when plotted as a function of time. Time is plotted along the horizontal direction, and the amplitude of the signal is plotted along the vertical direction.

SPECTRUM

The atom is the basic building block of matter—the sine wave is the basic building block of signals. A sine wave is a smoothly varying periodic signal. A sine wave sounds like a pure tone with no harmonic structure, such as the pure tones produced by a flute.

A sine wave has two important parameters: its maximum amplitude and its frequency. The frequency of a sine wave is the rate at which its basic shape—called a single cycle—repeats itself. Decades ago, frequency was expressed in the very descriptive units of cycles per second. Today, frequency is expressed in the more cryptic units of hertz (abbreviated Hz), after the nineteenth-century German physicist Heinrich Hertz. One hertz is the same as one cycle per second. For an audio signal, the higher its frequency, the higher its pitch; and the larger its maximum amplitude, the louder it sounds.

The eighteenth-century French mathematician Jean Baptiste Joseph Fourier showed that any complex signal can be decomposed into the sum of

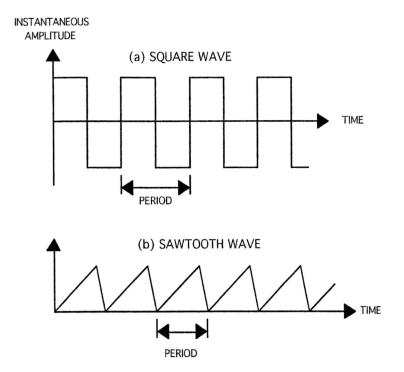

INSTANTANEOUS
AMPLITUDE

(a) SQUARE WAVE

TIME

PERIOD

(b) SAWTOOTH WAVE

TIME

PERIOD

FIGURE A.2
A periodic waveform has a basic shape that keeps repeating itself in time, such as
(a) the *square wave* and (b) the *sawtooth wave*, so named because of their shapes.
The length in time of this basic shape is called the *period* of the wave.

many sine waves with appropriate maximum amplitudes and frequencies.
The Fourier theorem is fundamental to the analysis of signals and waveforms. If a large number of sine waves were added together with each sine
wave having a frequency that was an odd multiple (or harmonic) of a fundamental frequency and also with a maximum amplitude inversely pro-
portional to the multiple, a square wave would be produced! Thus there are
two different ways of characterizing a signal or waveform: its actual shape
as a function of time, or the different frequencies that compose it. The first
way is called the *time domain*, and the second way is called the *frequency
domain*.

We can plot as a function of frequency the maximum amplitudes of the
different sine waves that compose a signal. Such a plot is called the *spectrum*

of the signal. Most signals occupy only a range or band of frequencies. The width of that range or band is called the *bandwidth* of the signal. A communication system, or communication channel, only transmits signals within a certain range or band. The width of the range of signals is called the *bandwidth* of the channel. Since the total bandwidth used by most communication systems is limited, the bandwidth of individual signals or channels determines the capacity of the system. The bandwidth of a communication system thus is a precious commodity.

SCIENTIFIC NOTATION

Engineers and scientists frequently work with a range of numbers from extremely large to extremely small, for example, 12,000,000 and 0.00000005. All these zeros can easily create a source of mistakes and errors. It is far easier to express these numbers as powers of 10. Such a system of expression is called scientific notation.

Exponents indicate the power of a number. For example, 10^3 is the same as $10 \times 10 \times 10$, or 1,000. A positive exponent indicates multiplication, and a negative exponent indicates division. Thus, 10^{-3} is the same as $1/(10 \times 10 \times 10)$, or 0.001. Using this scheme, we would write 12,000,000 as 12×10^6 and 0.00000005 as 5×10^{-8}.

Some powers of 10 appear so frequently, metric abbreviations are used instead. For example, 1,000 becomes a kilo, abbreviated as k. Thus, a frequency of 5,000 Hz is the same as 5 kHz. Table A.1 gives frequently used powers of 10 and the corresponding abbreviations.

Table A.1. Powers of 10.

1,000,000,000,000	10^{12}	tera (T)
1,000,000,000	10^{9}	giga (G)
1,000,000	10^{6}	mega (M)
1,000	10^{3}	kilo (k)
1	10^{0}	
0.001	10^{-3}	milli (m)
0.000001	10^{-6}	micro (μ)
0.000000001	10^{-9}	nano (n)
0.000000000001	10^{-12}	pico (p)

ELECTRICITY

Electricity is difficult to visualize, since like radio waves it cannot be seen. However, the effects of electricity are seen every time we turn on a lamp and are heard every time we listen to sound from a loudspeaker. What is electricity?

By its very name, electricity has to do with the flow of electrons. Electrons are negatively charged bundles of energy. Many metals and other substances have electrons that are free to move through the material, and hence such materials are good conductors of electricity. An electromotive force causes the electrons to flow, and the strength of an electromotive force is measured in volts. A battery uses chemical action to create an electromotive force. An electromotive force does not create electrons but simply creates a force to push or move electrons. Since the electromotive force does not create electrons, an endless supply of electrons is needed to create a steady flow through an electric conductor. The simplest way to create such an endless supply is to create a complete circuit.

One way to visualize electricity is to compare it to a bicycle chain. The chain forms a complete circuit about the pedal and wheel sprockets. When pedaling, a force moves the chain. Energy is transferred from the pedal to the wheel by the chain and the movement of the links in the chain. Each link pulls on the next; no new links are created, but rather an endless supply is created by the complete circuit of the chain around the two sprockets. The force of the pedal moves the links until they encounter the opposition, or resistance, of the wheel. The speed of the chain is determined by the pedal force and the opposition of the wheel. The speed of the chain could be measured by the number of links passing by in a second. Electrons are comparable to the links in the bicycle chain; the chain is comparable to the complete electric circuit; and the electromotive force is comparable to the force created by the pedal. The flow of electrons in an electric circuit encounters an opposition, or resistance, such as a light bulb or a motor, comparable to the wheel in the bicycle. The flow of electrons per second through the circuit is called the *electric current* and is measured in amperes. The electric opposition is measured in ohms.

A battery generates a constant electromotive force that does not vary with time; nor does it reverse direction. This steady electromotive force creates an electric current that likewise does not vary with time nor reverse direction. Such an electric current is called a *direct current*, or *DC*. An electromotive force could, however, vary in amplitude with time and might even change direction and would generate a similar time-varying electric current. Such a current is called an *alternating current*, or *AC*.

RADIO

Radio waves are baffling since we can neither see them nor feel them, yet they exist and travel through air and even the vacuum of space. We can hear and see their effects by listening to the radio and by watching television.

One way to understand and characterize radio waves is by describing them mathematically. The nineteenth-century Scottish physicist James Clerk Maxwell developed a set of equations for describing electromagnetic phenomena, such as light and radio waves. But his equations, although a powerful contribution to science, do little to help non-mathematicians visualize or understand radio waves. So let's try another way.

We have all experienced the effects of magnetism. We can hold a piece of metal near a magnet and can feel the magnetism attracting the metal. By moving the metal near the magnet, we can actually feel and sense the magnetic field that surrounds the magnet and that also extends far into space. Similarly, we might have combed our hair on a very dry day and felt the static electricity between the comb and our hair. This is an example of an electrostatic field that extends into space like a magnetic field. But what does all this have to do with radio?

When electricity flows in an electric circuit, magnetic and electrostatic fields are produced that extend far into space. If the flow of electricity is changing in direction and in amplitude, then the electromagnetic field likewise changes. The electricity thus creates an electromagnetic wave that extends far into space. The amplitude of the electromagnetic wave gets smaller as it travels greater and greater distances.

An antenna is a means of creating an electromagnetic wave from the changing flow of electricity. The electromagnetic wave is similar to the magnetic and electrostatic effects associated with magnets and static electricity. An *electromagnetic wave* is another name for what we know as a *radio wave*. If the flow of electricity is a sine wave, then the electromagnetic wave is also a sine wave. According to the antenna design and configuration, electromagnetic waves can be polarized to travel vertically, horizontally, or circularly.

Radio waves were discovered accidentally when an electric spark at one place created an electric spark nearby. Somehow the effect of the electric spark had traveled over distance, much to everyone's amazement. Electromagnetic waves had caused the effect. Today, we take radio waves for granted.

MODULATION

An audio signal, such as used in broadcast AM radio, occupies a band of frequencies from about 50 Hz to 5,000 Hz. The audio signal created by a telephone occupies a band of frequencies from about 300 to 3,500 Hz. A signal existing in its most basic form and occupying the range of frequencies as originally generated is called a *baseband signal*.

In broadcast radio, a number of separate radio stations all share the same overall band of frequencies. For example, the AM band in the United States extends from 535 kHz to 1,605 kHz. The only way this band of frequencies can be shared is to assign each radio station its own unique sub-band of frequencies within the AM band. This means that the baseband signal for each radio station must be shifted to a considerably higher frequency. Such frequency shifting is accomplished by modulation of a carrier wave. The carrier wave "carries" the baseband signal to a new range of frequencies. The baseband signal is otherwise unaffected by the process and can be recovered at the other end; the carrier wave thus is like a catalyst.

The carrier wave is a sine wave with a frequency equal to the center frequency of the specific band to which the baseband signal is to be shifted. Suppose a baseband signal is to be shifted to a sub-band located around 1,010 kHz. The carrier wave would have a frequency of 1,010 kHz. To accomplish frequency shifting through modulation, some property of the carrier wave must be varied in exact synchrony with the instantaneous amplitude variation of the baseband signal. If the maximum amplitude of the carrier wave is varied, the process is called *amplitude modulation*. If the frequency of the carrier wave is varied, the process is called *frequency modulation*. Modulation of the carrier wave occurs at the transmitter. The inverse process is called *demodulation*, and it occurs at the receiver.

With amplitude modulation, the maximum amplitude of a high-frequency sine wave—the carrier—is made to vary in synchrony with the instantaneous amplitude variation of the baseband, or modulating, signal. The positive maximum amplitude of the carrier looks exactly like the modulating signal. The effect of amplitude modulation is to shift the spectrum of the modulating signal to a new band of frequencies centered about the frequency of the carrier. The bandwidth of the amplitude-modulated carrier is exactly twice the bandwidth of the modulating signal. The spectrum of the modulated carrier consists of two portions: the upper sideband is a precise replica of the spectrum of the modulating signal and the lower sideband is its mirror image.

With frequency modulation, the instantaneous frequency of a high-frequency sine wave—the carrier—is made to vary in synchrony with the instantaneous amplitude variation of the baseband, or modulating, signal. The maximum amplitude of a frequency-modulated carrier remains constant. Like amplitude modulation, the effect of frequency modulation is to shift the spectrum of the modulating signal to a new band of frequencies centered about the frequency of the carrier. An upper sideband and a lower sideband are also created. However, the bandwidth of the frequency-modulated carrier is usually much more than just twice the bandwidth of the modulating signal.

Frequency modulation usually requires much more bandwidth than amplitude modulation. For example, the bandwidth of the baseband signal in broadcast AM radio is 5 kHz, and the bandwidth of an AM radio station is twice that, or 10 kHz. However, although the bandwidth of the baseband (nonstereo) signal in broadcast FM radio is 15 kHz, the bandwidth of an FM radio station is 200 kHz. The extra bandwidth used in frequency modulation results in an immunity to noise compared to amplitude modulation.

DIGITAL

The world as we humans sense it is a world in which sounds, sights, and other sensations vary continuously. This is a world in which measurement can never be totally precise. The alternative world is the digital world in which everything is represented as numbers, or strings of digits. This section explains the concept of digital.

Consider a concert performance in which the sound of the various musical instruments is sensed by a microphone. The output of the microphone is then recorded on magnetic tape and mass copied onto phonograph records and audiocassettes for sale to consumers. The recorded signal has a shape that is a replica of—or is analogous to—the original sound wave created by the musical instruments. Thus, the term *analog* is used to refer to the signal.

The output from the microphone is an electrical signal that continuously varies in synchrony with the acoustic signal generated by the musical instruments. The problem is that noise and distortion of the signal creeps into the recording and reproduction process, and the final signal listened to by the consumer is corrupted compared to the original signal. The digital process eliminates these problems.

With digital, the variation of the original signal is represented as a series of numbers, and the digits making up these numbers are encoded in binary form. All this will be made clearer by the following example, which explains the digital process in detail.

The output of a microphone is a continuously varying electrical signal. The signal varies with time, and at any instant in time, the signal can be any one of an infinite number of values in some range limited by some maximum value and some minimum value. We will assume that the output from our microphone varies between a minimum of –2 and a maximum of +2 volts.

The first step in converting the analog signal from the microphone to digital is to sample the analog signal in time. The Nyquist sampling theorem states that if we sample a signal at the appropriate rate, then the original signal can be recreated precisely with no loss of information. If the signal has a bandwidth of B Hz, then it must be sampled at least $2B$ times per second. For example, an audio signal with a bandwidth of 20,000 Hz needs to be sampled at least 40,000 times per second.

After sampling in time, the values of the signal at the sample times are quantized into a fixed number of intervals. Our signal ranges from –2 to +2 volts. Let us assume that we will quantize the signal into sixteen intervals. The first interval ranges from –2 to –1.75 volts, and the last, or sixteenth, interval ranges from +1.75 to +2 volts. The process of quantization reduces the detail in the signal, but if we choose a sufficient number of quantization intervals, the loss of detail will be acceptable. Upon reconstruction of the analog signal, we hear this loss of detail as quantization noise.

Our original audio signal is now represented as a series of numbers that represent the quantized levels of the sampled analog signal. Each quantized level is a two-digit decimal number: the first level is 00 and the last, or sixteenth, level is 15. The last step in the process is to encode each level as a binary number. Binary digits are either 0 or 1. The encoding of fifteen possibilities requires 4 binary digits, or bits for short. The decimal number 15 is 1111 in binary; 6 is 0110; 12 is 1100.

Our audio signal was sampled 40,000 times per second. Since each sample value has been encoded using 4 bits per sample, the overall bit rate for our audio digital signal is 160,000 bits per second. This digital signal can be encoded as an electrical signal for which one voltage level corresponds to a binary 0 and another voltage level corresponds to a binary 1. This encoded digital signal is itself an analog waveform that occupies bandwidth. The bandwidth of a digital signal is approximately one-half its bit rate. Our digitized audio signal of 160,000 bits per second would occupy a bandwidth of about 80,000 Hz.

Digital has conquered the world of audio with the compact disc and digital recording at the studio. Each channel of the stereophonic audio signal recorded on a compact disc is quantized into 65,536 levels using 16 bits to encode each level, and each channel is sampled 44,100 times per second. This relatively large number of bits per sample assures that the quantized signal is a near perfect replica of the original analog waveform. The world of telephony has also been conquered by digital. Telephone signals, however, do not require the high quality of the compact disc. Telephone signals have a bandwidth of about 4,000 Hz and are sampled 8,000 times per second. Only 256 levels are used to quantize them using 8 bits to encode each level. The bit rate for telephone signals is 64,000 bits per second.

TRANSMISSION MEDIA

A variety of transmission media convey communication signals from one place to another. Electric signals are carried over twisted pairs of copper wires and over coaxial cable. Coaxial cable consists of an inner conductor surrounded by a shield that is also a conductor—hence the term *coaxial*. Radio waves carry signals from one location to another. Very high frequency radio waves, called *microwaves*, are used to carry telephone signals from the antenna on one tower to another. A series of such microwave towers, spaced about twenty-six miles apart, used to carry telephone signals across the country.

Communication satellites are located 22,300 miles above the earth's equator. At this distance, the satellite takes exactly twenty-four hours to complete an orbit and thus appears stationary with respect to the surface of the earth beneath it. Such an orbit is called a *geostationary orbit*. A communication satellite simply receives a radio signal from Earth, amplifies it, and then retransmits it back to Earth, slightly changing its radio frequency to prevent interference. The circuitry in the satellite that performs this is called a transponder. Typically, a communication satellite has twenty-four transponders and thus is able to handle twenty-four separate radio channels. The main problem with the use of satellites for telephone communication is the delay that occurs for the radio signal to travel from Earth to the satellite and back. However, satellites are great for sending television signals from one coast to another, since such broadcast communication is one-way and the delay is not a problem.

The newest transmission medium is optical fiber. Actually the basic concept is over a hundred years old, but it required modern technology to manufacture glass (silica) fibers pure enough for practical use. An optical fiber acts like a mirrored tube and continuously reflects any light that is shined into it. In the world of optical fiber, thin is in, and the thinnest fiber (about a tenth the diameter of a human hair) has the highest signal-carrying capacity since all the light rays travel parallel to each other. A small laser is used to generate the light beam. Laser light has a single frequency (monochromatic), all the rays are parallel to each other (collimated), and all the rays vibrate together in perfect synchrony (coherent). A detector at the output end of the fiber senses the light signal and creates a corresponding electric signal. The light beam is simply turned on and off to send a digital signal.

Optical fiber has tremendous capacity. A single light channel on an optical fiber can carry three million digital telephone signals, or four thousand TV channels. The state of the art continues to advance, and these capacities will likewise increase, in particular with the use of multiple light channels on a single fiber—a technique called wave-division multiplexing.

The twisted pairs of copper wires, called the *local loop*, that carry telephone signals to our homes and offices still convey analog signals. Perhaps some day in the near future the telephone instrument itself along with the signals carried over the local loop will be digital, just like the signals carried over the telephone network today. Whether a new transmission medium to the home, such as optical fiber, will be needed or exactly how this total conversion of telephone service to digital will be accomplished remains unclear at the present. Also still unresolved is whether the same optical fiber to the home used for telephone signals will also carry the television signals of today's CATV industry. As you can well imagine, the telephone companies and the CATV companies have quite different views of who will own and control the fiber, if a single fiber to the home is installed.

SWITCHING
One aspect of interpersonal communication that makes it unique compared to broadcast communication is its one-on-one nature. With telephone service

we are able to reach and communicate with any other person by telephone. What makes this possible is the switched public telephone network.

Switching can be accomplished in two ways: space-division switching and time-division switching. With space-division switching, a complete path or circuit is connected between the two parties for the complete duration of the telephone call. A simple on-off switch can open or close an electric circuit. A rotary switch can connect one to one of many. A matrix switch can connect various inputs to outputs. In years past, the actual contacts where the connections were made were electromechanical. Today, transistors act as electronic switches and make the electrical connections.

With time-division switching, the order of samples on a time-division-multiplexed medium are rearranged. This rearrangement, or reordering, sends the sample value from one telephone circuit to another circuit. The actual device that performs this reordering is called a *time-slot interchange unit*.

In the old days of telephone switching, human operators made the connections between calling parties. Today, switching is automated. A modern telephone switching machine consists of two parts: the switch where the actual connections are made and the computer that controls the switch. Most switching machines today use time-division switching and are called *digital switching machines* since the interchanged and reordered sample values are digital signals.

The control computers in the switching machines that make up the telephone network need to communicate with each other so that the appropriate connections from one telephone to another are made. This aspect of the operation of the telephone network is called *signaling*. The control computers communicate with each other over a dedicated data network, called the *signaling network*.

When you pick up the telephone handset, direct current (DC) flows through the wires connecting your telephone to the nearest serving office. That flow of DC is sensed by the switching machine in your telephone company's central office. The machine thus knows that you want service, and the machine returns a dial tone to you. You then dial the number of the party you wish to call. Each time you push a button on your touchtone telephone, a unique combination of two tones is generated, and equipment at the central office can decode the digit you have dialed. When you have dialed all the digits of the number, the switching machine examines the number and initiates a sequence of steps to make the final connection. If the call is long distance, the number is sent to the nearest switching machine of your chosen long-distance company. This signaling information is sent over a dedicated data network, called *common channel signaling*. The number is then used to make a connection to wherever you have dialed. The number is finally sent to the local switching machine at the distant end, and the last connection to the called party is made. An electric signal is sent down the line to the called party's telephone to make it ring. The called party lifts the handset, DC flows, and the called party's local office knows the party has answered the phone. The connection is now complete and talking commences. What is amazing is that all this happens in a few seconds and with such ease that we take quality telephone service for granted.

The telephone network is an example of a circuit-, or line-, switched network. When you make a telephone call, a circuit dedicated to your call is created and maintained for the full duration of your call, even if you and the other party commune together simply by silent meditation. Circuit switching is fine for voice communication, but computer communication consists of short bursts and is served best by another form of switching called packet switching. With packet switching, a data message is divided into a number of packets, usually all of the same number of bits (typically about 1,000 bits). In addition to containing the actual message, each packet also has a header that gives the address of the destination in a computer meaningful form. The packet is sent along the network, gradually moving toward the destination, in a fashion similar to the way switches are thrown as a railroad train makes its way to its destination. Packet switching is the method used for the Internet.

TELEVISION

The concept of scanning an image is basic to the workings of television and also facsimile. An image is a two-dimensional representation of a scene or object. A signal, however, varies in only one dimension as a function of time. Scanning is the process of converting two dimensions into one.

The television camera is an image scanner. It scans very rapidly across the image in a horizontal direction starting at the left and moving to the right. At the same time, the scanning element moves relatively slowly from the top to the bottom of the image. Each horizontal scan across the image is called a *scan line*. Increasing the total number of scan lines for an image increases the resolution or spatial detail. The output of the TV camera is an electrical signal that varies with the brightness of the image as it is scanned.

The television image is recreated at the TV set on the picture tube—the cathode ray tube, or CRT. A beam of electrons forms a spot and is swept quickly across the CRT screen from left to right and more slowly from top to bottom. As the strength of the beam is varied, the brightness of the reproducing spot on the screen likewise varies. The scan and sweep rates are so fast that the human eye does not see individual sweep lines but rather sees a complete two-dimensional image. Each image, or frame, is scanned and reproduced at a rate such that the individual frames fuse together into a continuous experience, just like the individual frames of a motion picture fuse together to create the experience of continuous motion. For television in the United States, the frames are sent at a rate of about 30 frames per second. Each individual frame is scanned 525 times at a rate of about 15,750 lines per second.

The scan rate at the camera and the sweep rate at the TV set need to be precisely synchronized. This is accomplished by the transmission of sharp pulses at the beginning of each horizontal scan line. The TV receiver searches for these pulses and synchronizes itself to them thereby assuring synchronization. These pulses are called *horizontal synchronization pulses*.

The beam at the CRT needs time to retrace its path and position itself at the top of the screen to begin the next frame. A vertical synchronization pulse is transmitted to cause this to occur. The beam is turned off, or blanked, during the vertical retrace interval to be certain it is not visible.

The cathode ray tube in a color television receiver has three electron beams corresponding to the three additive primary colors of red, blue, and green. If you look closely at the screen of a color CRT, you can see all the small dots of primary colors that form the color image. The great engineering feat was devising a method for transmitting the additional information necessary for creating a color image while maintaining compatibility with existing monochrome (black-and-white) TV sets. How this was achieved by the National Television System Committee (NTSC) in the early 1950s is beyond this book.

A baseband television signal has a maximum frequency of about 4.2 MHz. The video signal is sent over the air using amplitude modulation of the radio-frequency carrier. The audio signal is sent separately using frequency modulation of a separate audio carrier. Since the video and audio signals are sent separately, the video portion might fail but you can still hear the audio, or vice versa. The total bandwidth of the baseband video and audio signal is 4.5

MHz. The total bandwidth of a broadcast television channel after appropriate modulation of the carriers is 6 MHz.

The 525 scan lines and video bandwidth of 4.2 MHz were chosen to match the resolution of human vision for a viewing distance that is about four times the height of the picture on the screen. For large-screen TV sets and for small TV sets viewed closely, higher resolution or definition in the image might be needed, perhaps a doubling of the number of scan lines to about 1,000. A conventional TV image is a little wider than it is high by the ratio 4:3; this aspect ratio might be increased to about 5:3 to create a wide-screen viewing experience. This high-definition TV (HDTV) requires a new technical standard, and a whole new digital standard is emerging for the future.

Digital television involves the conversion of the video information to a digital format. Since the video signal occupies considerable bandwidth, converting it to a digital format results in a very high bit rate—as high as hundreds of millions of bits per second. But there is considerable redundancy in video, both within each frame and between frames. Digital compression can reduce the bit rate for digital television to a few million bits per second, requiring practical amounts of bandwidth.

Broadcast television signals are transmitted over the air as radio waves. Channels 2 through 13 in the United States are sent in the very high frequency (VHF) band from 54 Mhz to 216 Mhz; channels 14 through 69 are sent in the ultra high frequency (UHF) band from 470 MHz to 806 MHz. Television signals are also sent over coaxial cable—a system known as *CATV*. Although the *CA* today is taken to stand for *coaxial*, it originally stood for *community antenna*: a rural community would erect a tall antenna, receive TV stations from a distant city, and then retransmit the TV stations over a coaxial cable to each home in the community. The coaxial cable used by the CATV firm is a one-way broadcast medium capable of carrying as many as a hundred TV signals. In the future, CATV firms will be using optical fiber to replace coaxial cable in more and more portions of their distribution system to the home.

HIGH FIDELITY AND STEREO

The phonograph of Edison's day had poor sound quality, and a listener had to strain to understand what was being said or sung. The use of modern electronics changed all that and resulted in a high fidelity that approached actually being at a concert or performance. The effect of realism is further increased through the use of stereophonic (stereo) techniques in which two separate signals are recorded and reproduced through two separate loudspeakers or headphones: a left channel and a right channel.

FM stereo was an exciting advance in technology since the additional information for two separate signals could be transmitted and yet be compatible with earlier single-channel FM radio receivers. This was accomplished by adding together the left and right signals (L + R) and then sending this sum signal like a regular FM radio signal, and the sum signal if received by an older nonstereo radio receiver would sound acceptable. A stereo difference signal was formed by subtracting the right signal from the left signal (L − R). The stereo difference signal was then sent along with the sum signal. A stereo radio receiver would receive both signals, and by adding and subtracting them would generate the separate left and right signals, for example, (L + R) + (L − R) = 2L.

An important advance in the world of recorded sound was magnetic tape recording. The surface of magnetic tape is formed of many very small particles, or slivers, of iron oxide, or some other ferrous material. These slivers when magnetized by a magnetic field retain the magnetism. A varying electric current flowing through a coil of wire generates a varying magnetic field. By placing this varying magnetic field near the magnetic tape, the tape becomes magnetized as it passes by the coil of wire and retains the changing pattern of magnetism. If the tape is moved past a coil of wire, a varying electric current is generated that matches the original magnetizing signal. A stereo tape recorder has two coils of wire, called record heads, that record two separate signals: a left channel and a right channel. Each stereo signal has its own track on the tape. Magnetic tape recording is subject to wear and tear, the magnetism slowly fades over time, and noise in the form of residual magnetism is heard whenever the tape is played.

Television signals have considerably more bandwidth than high-fidelity audio signals. Recording television signals thus is not that simple. Indeed, the home videocassette recorder is a sophisticated device.

The world of high fidelity has been revolutionized by the use of digital technology to record concerts and performances. The digital signal thus recorded is a series of digits that can always be recreated perfectly, thereby assuring that the original recording will never deteriorate. The compact disc (CD) contains a replica of the original recorded digital signal. The CD is read by a beam of laser light and thus will never wear out, unlike magnetic tape, which must rub across the record/playback head, and the phonograph record, which must be traced by a mechanical stylus.

COMPUTERS AND MODEMS

Any retrospective of the twenty-first century will most certainly view the computer as one of its major accomplishments. We truly cannot escape the impact of computers on our daily lives. Our paychecks, grades, airline reservations, taxes, cars, and credit are a few of the items controlled by computers. The watches we wear on our wrists most likely contain a small computer. We type our term papers and correspondence on a computer.

A computer is an electronic machine that is capable of performing arithmetic calculations and other operations on various types of numeric and alphabetic data with astonishing speed and with perfect accuracy. A computer is a general-purpose machine that can be instructed or programmed to perform different operations or functions. A computer consists of the machine itself along with various input devices (such as a keyboard) and output devices (such as a visual display or a printer). These physical components of a computer are called hardware. In addition to hardware, a computer requires a set of instructions, or a program, to tell it precisely what to do (such as in playing a game or processing words). The computer program is called *software.*

Clearly, the perfect accuracy of a computer and its fast speed of operation are important advantages. However, its unique advantage is its flexibility: according to the specific software used, a computer can do many different things for the user. The same computer can be used to process words as a sophisticated typewriter (word processing) or can be used to perform sophisticated calculations on tables of data (spreadsheet calculation). Large databases of information can be categorized, sorted, and accessed (database programs).

A computer is a binary machine in that it stores and uses binary information in its operation and calculations. Thus, the 0 and 1 of the bit is the most fundamental unit of information used in a computer. By assigning unique combinations of bits to alphabetic and numeric characters, text can be represented, stored, and processed by a computer. The American Standard Code for Information Interchange (ASCII) uses 8 bits to encode alphanumeric characters for use by computers. A *byte* is another name for the 8 bits used to encode a character.

Decades ago computers were physically huge and filled a large room. Compared to today's computers, these machines were incredibly slow and costly. Today, all and much more of the processing power of these early computers is contained on a single microprocessor chip of silicon less than one inch square.

The program that controls the computer consists of a series of instructions. Each instruction is performed one by one in sequence by the computer. Instructions tell the computer to retrieve data stored in its memory, to process this data in some way, to store the results back in memory, and to print numbers. The computer is able to process millions of such instructions in a second. The memory of a computer can store hundred of thousands and even millions of bytes of data.

Computers can be used as terminals to access data stored in remote databases. This remote access is frequently made using the telephone network. However, computers utilize digital data in the form of on-off bits, but the telephone network conveys signals in the form of tones. Thus, conversion is needed from the bits of the computer to the tones of the telephone network. The bits modulate a tone for transmission over the telephone network; the tone is demodulated to obtain the bits required by the computer. The device situated between the computer and the telephone line that performs this modulation and demodulation is called a *modem*.

Voice telephone signals can also be broken into packets and sent over the Internet—a technology known as *voice over the Internet protocol*, or *VoIP*. A high-speed Internet connection is required for VoIP. Such high-speed—or broadband—Internet access is accomplished over either a cable modem that utilizes a broadband channel on the coaxial cable of the CATV company or a digital subscriber line (DSL) modem that works over the twisted-pair of the telephone company.

REFERENCES

Noll, A. Michael. *Principles of Modern Communications Technology.* Norwood, Mass.: Artech House, 2001.

Pierce, John R., and A. Michael Noll. *SIGNALS: The Science of Telecommunication.* New York: Scientific American Books, 1990.

Bibliography

Agee, Warren K., Phillip H. Ault, and Edwin Emery. *Introduction to Mass Communications.* 10th ed. New York: HarperCollins, 1991.

Anderson, Robert H., et al. *Universal Access to E-Mail: Feasibility and Societal Implications.* Santa Monica, Calif.: RAND, 1995.

Ball-Rokeach, Sandra, and Kathleen Reardon. "Monologue, Dialogue, and Telelog: Comparing an Emerging Form of Communication with Traditional Forms." In *Advancing Communication Science: Merging Mass and Interpersonal Processes,* edited by Robert P. Hawkins et al. Newbury Park, Calif.: Sage, 1988, 136–161.

Bohlin, Erik, Karolina Brodin, Anders Lundgren, and Bertil Thorngren, eds. *Convergence in Communications and Beyond.* Amsterdam: Elsevier, 2000.

Bretz, Rudy. *A Taxonomy of Communication Media.* Englewood Cliffs, N.J.: Educational Technology Publications, 1971.

Brooks, John. *Telephone: The First Hundred Years.* New York: Harper & Row, 1975.

Ciampa, John A. *Communication: The Living End.* New York: Philosophical Library, 1988.

Collis, David J., P. William Bane, and Stephen P. Bradley. "Winners and Losers." In *Competing in the Age of Digital Convergence,* edited by David B. Yoffie. Boston: Harvard Business School Press, 1997, 159–200.

Condry, John. *The Psychology of Television.* Mahwah, N.J.: Lawrence Erlbaum, 1989.

DeFleur, Melvin L., and Everette E. Dennis. *Understanding Mass Communication.* 2nd ed. Boston: Houghton Mifflin Company, 1985.

Dizard, Wilson, Jr. *Old Media New Media: Mass Communications in the Information Age.* White Plains, N.Y.: Longman, 1994.

Douglas, Susan J. *Inventing American Broadcasting: 1899–1922.* Baltimore: John Hopkins University Press, 1987.

Fisher, David E., and Marshall Jon Fisher. *Tube: The Invention of Television.* Washington, D.C.: Counterpoint, 1996.

Gates, Bill. *The Road Ahead.* New York: Vintage Books, 1995.

Goldstein, Fred R. *The Great Telecom Meltdown.* Norwood, Mass.: Artech House, 2005.

Huxley, Aldous. *Brave New World.* New York: Doubleday, 1932.

Innis, Harold A. *The Bias of Communication.* Toronto: University of Toronto Press, 1951.

Isom, Warren Rex, ed. "The Phonograph and Sound Recording after One-Hundred Years." *Journal of the Audio Engineering Society* 25, no. 10/11 (October/November 1977).

Jean, Georges. *Writing: The Story of Alphabets and Scripts.* New York: Harry N. Abrams, 1992.

Lewis, Tom. *Empire of the Air: The Men Who Made Radio.* New York: Edward Burlingame Books, 1991.

"Losing the HP Way." *Economist* 372, no. 8389 (August 21, 2004): 49–50.

Luplow, Wayne, ed. "A History of Consumer Electronics: Commemorating a Century of Electrical Progress." *IEEE Transactions on Consumer Electronics* CE-30, no. 2 (May 1984).

Mackay, James. *Alexander Graham Bell: A Life.* New York: John Wiley & Sons, 1997.

McLaughlin, John F., with Anne Louise Antonoff. "Mapping the Information Business." Program on Information Resources Policy. Cambridge: Harvard University, 1986.

McLuhan, Marshall. *Understanding Media: The Extensions of Man.* New York: McGraw Hill, 1964. Reprinted by MIT Press, 1994.

McLuhan, Marshall, and Quentin Fiore. *The Medium Is the Massage: An Inventory of Effects.* New York: Bantam Books, 1962.

Melosi, Martin V. *Thomas A. Edison and the Modernization of America.* New York: HarperCollins, 1990.

Miller, George A. *The Science of Words*. New York: Scientific American Library, 1991.

Negroponte, Nicholas. *Being Digital*. New York: Vintage Books, 1995.

Newhouse, Elizabeth L., ed. *Inventors and Discoverers: Changing Our World*. Washington, D.C.: National Geographic Society, 1988.

Noam, Eli, Jo Groebel, and Darcy Gerbarg. *Internet Television*. Mahwah, N.J.: Lawrence Erlbaum, 2004.

Noll, A. Michael. "Man-Machine Tactile Communication." *SID Journal* 1, no. 2 (July/August 1972): 5–11.

———. "Anatomy of a Failure: Picturephone Revisited." *Telecommunication Policy* 16, no. 4 (May/June 1992): 307–316.

———. *Highway of Dreams: A Critical View along the Information Superhighway*. Mahwah, N.J.: Lawrence Erlbaum, 1997.

———. *Principles of Modern Communications Technology*. Norwood, Mass.: Artech House, 2001.

Pember, Don R. *Mass Media in America*. 5th ed. Chicago: Science Research Associates, 1987.

Pierce, John R., and A. Michael Noll. *SIGNALS: The Science of Telecommunication*. New York: Scientific American Books, 1990.

Pretzer, William S., ed. *Working at Inventing: Thomas A. Edison and the Menlo Park Experience*. Baltimore, Md.: Johns Hopkins University Press, 2002.

Rhoads, Christopher. "Bringing Fiber Home." *Wall Street Journal*, August 19, 2004, B1–B2.

Robichaux, Mark. "Highway of Hype." *Wall Street Journal*, November 29, 1993, A7.

Robinson, David. *From Peep Show to Palace: The Birth of American Film*. New York: Columbia University Press, 1996.

Salvaggio, Jerry L., ed. *The Information Society: Economic, Social, and Structural Issues*. Mahwah, N.J.: Lawrence Erlbaum, 1989.

Schramm, Wilbur. "Channels and Audiences." In *Handbook of Communication*, edited by Ithiel de Sola Pool et al. Chicago: Rand McNally, 1973, 160–174.

———. *The Story of Human Communication*. New York: Harper & Row, 1988.

Shannon, Claude E. "A Mathematical Theory of Communication." *Bell System Technical Journal* 27 (1948): 379–423, 623–656.

Sigel, Efrem, ed. *Videotext: The Coming Revolution in Home/Office Information Retrieval.* New York: Harmony Books, 1980.

Singleton, Loy A. *Telecommunications in the Information Age.* 2nd ed. Cambridge, Mass.: Ballinger, 1986.

Straubhaar, Joseph, and Robert LaRose. *Communications in the Information Society.* Belmont, Calif.: Wadsworth, 1997.

Tydeman, John, et al. *Teletext and Videotex in the United States: Market Potential, Technology, Public Policy Issues.* New York: McGraw Hill, 1982.

Valovic, Thomas S. *Digital Mythologies: The Hidden Complexities of the Internet.* New Brunswick, N.J.: Rutgers University Press, 2000.

Wang, William S-Y, ed. *Human Communication: Language and Its Psychobiological Bases.* New York: W. H. Freeman, 1982.

———. *Language, Writing, and the Computer.* New York: W. H. Freeman, 1986.

Whetmore, Edward Jay. *Mediamerica: Form, Content, and Consequence of Mass Communication.* 4th ed. Belmont, Calif.: Wadsworth, 1991.

Winsbury, Rex. *The Electronic Bookstall: Push-Button Publishing on Videotex.* London: International Institute of Communications, 1979.

Zarem, Abe. Foreword to *Highway of Dreams: A Critical View along the Information Superhighway,* by A. Michael Noll. Mahwah, N.J.: Lawrence Erlbaum, 1997, iii–vi.

Index

About the Author

A. **Michael Noll** is professor emeritus of communications at the Annenberg School for Communication at the University of Southern California and was dean of the school for an interim period from 1992 to 1994. Noll spent nearly fifteen years performing basic research at Bell Labs and is one of the earliest pioneers in the use of digital computers in the visual arts. In the early 1970s, he was on the staff of the president's science adviser at the White House and later worked at AT&T identifying opportunities for new products and services. Noll is affiliated with the Columbia Institute for Tele-Information at Columbia University and the Media Center at New York Law School. He has published over ninety professional papers and over one hundred editorial and other short pieces. He holds six patents and has written nine books on various aspects of telecommunication and has edited a book on crisis communication. He also writes reviews of classical music performances and is quoted frequently in the media.